PURE HEART
ENLIGHTENED MIND

The Zen Journal and Letters of
Maura "Soshin" O'Halloran

by

Maura O'Halloran

Introduction by Ruth O'Halloran
Afterword by Dai-En Bennage
Illustrations by Elizabeth O'Halloran

RIVERHEAD BOOKS, NEW YORK

Excerpts from "In Twenty-Seven Short Years: The Enlightenment of Maura O'Halloran" by Ruth O'Halloran, *Commonweal*, February 28, 1992, are used by permission of the publisher.

Riverhead Books
Published by The Berkley Publishing Group
200 Madison Avenue
New York, New York 10016

Charles E. Tuttle Co., Inc., edition published 1994
Riverhead edition: October 1995

Library of Congress Cataloging-in-Publication Data

O'Halloran, Maura, 1955–1982.
    Pure heart, enlightened mind: the Zen journal and letters of Maura "Soshin" O'Halloran / by Maura O'Halloran; introduction by Ruth O'Halloran, afterword by Dai–En Bennage; illustrations by Elizabeth O'Halloran.
        p. cm.
    Originally published: Boston: Charles E. Tuttle Co., 1994.
    ISBN 1-57322-503-7
    1. O'Halloran, Maura, 1955–1982.   2. Spiritual life—Zen Buddhism.
I. Title.
BQ976.H35A3   1995
294.3'927'092—dc20   95–22765
[B]   CIP

Printed in the United States of America

10   9   8   7   6   5   4   3   2   1

From the reviews of *Pure Heart, Enlightened Mind: The Zen Journal and Letters of Maura "Soshin" O'Halloran*:

"Religion, suggested Nietzsche, is the last refuge of weaklings and cowards. But the truth is otherwise: one thinks of Gandhi facing a line of British clubs or Thomas More venturing one last quip as he awaits the executioner's ax. There is another kind of spiritual courage as well, quieter and less celebrated, but just as remarkable: that of making each day, in its most conventional aspects—cooking, eating, breathing—an oblation to the absolute. Of such bravery, cast in this instance in the Buddhist mold, is the brief and moving life of Maura O'Halloran . . . a compelling story . . . O'Halloran explores an unfamiliar country and unknown regions of the soul."
—*New York Times Book Review*

"A fascinating picture of an Irish-American girl dropped in the midst of a male monastery in Japan in the late 1970s. One shivers at her descriptions of begging in the snow, cooking and cleaning while adjusting to both the traditional disciplines and to the mercurial characters of fellow monks. What a victory when she received ordination, after two years, much work, and a few puzzling enlightenments. And what a mystery when her life was cut short at age 27 by a tragic accident. This account, in journal entries and letters home, should become a classic in the Zen literature involving Westerners."
—*Library Journal*

"Through her most private and heartfelt words, Maura eloquently describes the rigors, hardships, and ultimate joys of Zen training and temple life . . . throughout all her writings, an endless sense of love and compassion is revealed. *Pure Heart, Enlightened Mind* will touch all those who read it. It will quickly become a classic of Zen study along the lines of *The Three Pillars of Zen* and *Zen Mind, Beginner's Mind*. More that that, it will serve as a lasting tribute to a woman who, in the words inscribed on her statue in Japan, was 'a real incarnation of Kannon Bosatsu to be loved and respected forever.'"
—*Asian Pages*

Contents

Publisher's Note

The material for this book arrived at our offices in November of 1992. Since then we have struggled to determine how best to present these letters and journals of Maura *Soshin* O'Halloran.

Journals are inherently incomplete things, for the most fundamental issues of a life or an experience are understood by the writer and are often unwritten. Because of this, Maura's journals present us with many questions that remain unanswered—why did she want to study Zen, why did she go to Japan, what elements of her Catholic upbringing led her to Buddhism? We asked Maura's family and the people with whom she studied and, ultimately, the only answers are here in these pages before you. Maura never intended this material to be published. Whatever questions we may have after reading these, her most personal thoughts, are not questions that were most important to Maura. What was important to her was that she become a Zen monk and be able to help other people in some way. This is what mattered to her.

Japanese words are used throughout the text. The first time a Japanese word appears it will be printed in italics with an explanation. It will be romanized thereafter.

We wish to acknowledge Ruth O'Halloran's dedication in transcribing her daughter's writings for publication. She was helped by Kate, Scott, and Elizabeth O'Halloran. I wish to thank Tetsugyu Ban, Tessai-san, and Shiro Tachibana for welcoming me to Kannonji Temple and transmitting to me their love for Maura-san. I am also grateful to Paul Silverman, Lorette Zirker, and Dai-en Bennage for their insight and editorial guidance.

This book is dedicated to Maura *Soshin* O'Halloran.

—Michael Kerber, Editor

Introduction

 In a small Buddhist monastery in northern Japan there stands a statue of a young Irish-American woman who lived there in the early 1980s. During her three years of Zen training in Iwate and Tokyo she was known as Maura-san, or by her monastic name of Soshin-san. She received the transmission of her roshi in 1982 and was killed in a bus accident in Thailand six months later. In 1983, as her mother, I was invited to Japan for the dedication of her Kannon statue, an indication that she had become identified in the minds of local people with the bodhisattva Kannon, the Buddhist saint of compassion.

Her last photo, taken in front of a Bangkok temple just before she boarded a bus which crashed on the road to Chiang Mai, shows a tall, blue-eyed, black-robed young woman of twenty-seven, with a radiant smile. How did this daughter of an American mother and an Irish father, educated at convent schools and Trinity College, Dublin, become not only a Zen monk but a Buddhist saint?

Maura O'Halloran was born on May 24th, 1955, in Boston, Massachusetts, the eldest of six children. Her father, Fionan Finbarr O'Halloran, was a native of County Kerry, Ireland, and I, her mother, am a native of Maine. When Maura was four years old we moved to Ireland. Her earliest schooling was at Loretto convents in County Dublin. She briefly attended the same school as Mother Teresa and had hoped to meet her when she went to India after her travels in Thailand. Maura had expressed an intention of doing similar work to Mother Teresa's among the poor of Dublin.

We returned to Boston in 1966, living in suburban Waban while my husband did graduate work in civil engineering at M.I.T. He was killed in a road accident in 1969 and the entire family returned to Dublin in 1970.

In her journal, Maura never mentions the fact of her birth and youth in Boston, but her New England background, and especially her grandmother in Maine, contributed as much to her formation as did her fourteen years in Ireland. Her position as the eldest child, flung into the role of second parent to five younger siblings at her father's sudden death, hastened a maturity that few adolescents experience.

After receiving high honors in her Leaving Certificate from her secondary school in Ireland, she gained early acceptance at Trinity College, Dublin, where she matriculated in 1973. In 1975 she received Ireland's highest scholastic award, the Foundation Scholarship at Trinity College, which provided for all her educational expenses. She continued to do outstanding scholastic work until 1977 when she completed her joint degrees in mathematical economics/statistics and in sociology. As a mathematician and linguist she distinguished herself in school, but as a compassionate and wise human being she early gave promise of a rare spirituality. While in college she did much volunteer social work, especially with drug addicts and the very poor of Dublin. She spent the summer of 1976 at the Rudolph Steiner School in Glengraig, Northern Ireland, where she cared for autistic and retarded children.

Her highly developed sense of the need for social justice sometimes made her impatient with institutional obstacles to human development. This point of view found an outlet in college protests, volunteer social work, union organizing (she antagonized the management of a restaurant in which she worked in Dublin by attempting to organize the staff into a union) and what I can only call a sort of spontaneous poverty. The latter attitude led to such a detachment from material things, especially fashionable clothing, that she often appeared genuinely shabby (years before the current vogue for "shabby chic"). She deliberately limited herself to a very stringent budget.

Over her college vacations she made a series of journeys through Greece, Italy, North Africa, France and the United Kingdom. In the summer of 1977 she returned to the United States and then went to Toronto, Canada, where she worked at several jobs to earn money for cross-continental travel. She drove with friends across Canada, then worked her way down the west coast until she arrived in San Francisco. There she worked at several jobs simultaneously (waitress, hotel desk clerk, telephone operator and research assistant). She also studied photography and Spanish to prepare for a major trip through Latin America.

Describing this trip, she says:

Starting in April, 1978, I travelled through Mexico, Central America and most of South America, remaining in Cuzco, Peru, for almost five months where I taught English and improved my Spanish. [She also did volunteer social work in Cuzco.] My lifestyle while travelling brought me into contact with people from every social level. I hitch-hiked, walked or travelled second-class, as did the Indians. People, from local campesinos to wealthy hacienda owners, continually showed me hospitality, bringing me to their homes and talking for long hours about their lives, problems, politics and ambitions.

She ventured as far south as Punta da Arenas and flew back from Santiago, Chile, arriving in Maine in the midst of a blizzard on Christmas Day, 1978.

After a visit with her family, who had moved back to Maine from Ireland earlier in 1978, she went to Boston where she lived in a studio apartment on Bromfield Street while working at a Cambridge restaurant to finance her proposed trip to the Orient. In Boston she became active in the anti-nuclear movement and continued her study of photography, which culminated in a one-man show of her work in 1979. Her interest in Japan had been aroused by the enthusiasm of the family's old friend and solicitor in Ireland, Frank Sweeney, and by her own long-term interest in meditation. In our Dublin home in the early 1970s one often came upon her in some corner, sitting in the lotus position, calmly centered within herself, oblivious to phone, TV, and family. She had the ability to focus cheerfully and totally on whatever she did and I have no doubt that this was partly the result of her habit of meditation.

Her last month of living in America was September, 1979, which she spent writing, reading and thinking in her Aunt Anne's lake-side cottage at much loved Wayne, Maine. After a week spent with friends in San Francisco, she flew to Hawaii and then to Tokyo.

Her journals and letters take the narrative from this point. The following are excerpts from the notebooks and journals kept by Maura O'Halloran during the period of her three years' training in Zen at Toshoji Temple in Tokyo and Kannonji Temple in Iwate Prefecture, Japan, 1979–1982. The roshi of these temples is Tetsugyu Ban.

—Ruth O'Halloran

PRELUDE

Dear Family,

Well, the luck of the Irish stayed intact across the international dateline, and I'm doing great. Sure and begorra, let me tell you the tricks.

First off, I arrive in Honolulu at two in the morning and I'm exhausted and bleary-eyed (having, of course, been up with friends in San Francisco most of the night before). So I try to find somewhere to lay my head before trying to track down cousin Ed. I ended up under a palm tree amidst all these bushes, crooking myself in and out of its sinuous roots. Hardly the Hilton, but it does till dawn. Then, stumbling and staggering, I phone a million different numbers only to find that cousin Ed is out at sea. At that stage I'd do anything for a bit of sleep, and that's where my next adventure begins.

When you picture me in Hawaii, do you see me in a bikini on Waikiki Beach, sipping piña coladas? Try envisioning me in a sari, at a Hare Krishna temple, explaining how to make Irish potato bread. That's it. In the airport I got chatting with a girl named Nancy, a recent convert who'd do anything for Krishna, including giving shelter to a poor Irish waif. Well, I ended up there for nearly a week, scrubbing pots and cooking in exchange for my keep. And did I learn a lot about the Krishnas! (To get away, I had to pretend I was leaving for one of their other temples.) They dressed me up in a sari and proceeded to try to convert me. We got up every morning at 3:00 A.M. for service and a Bhagavad Gita lesson. This involved singing, dancing, chanting, and making offerings to the deities—all very pretty, but at three in the morning I was less than enthused. Then we go off to chant our rounds before the sunrise, 16 rounds of 109 beads, each one requiring "Hare Krishna, Hare Krishna, Krishna, Krishna, Hare, Hare, Hare Rama, Hare Rama, Rama, Rama, Hare, Hare." Now let me hear you say that fast, 1,744 times (before breakfast). I developed the knack of curling up in a little niche in the largest banyan tree in Hawaii and grabbing a bit of a snooze.

They start from the premise that the world is a place of misery, is an illusion—maya—a mere unsatisfactory reflection of the real and wonderful world in which Krishna dwells. In order to free themselves from endless reincarnations, they seek to deny themselves any sense of gratification, sublimating all pleasures for the desire to be with Krishna. So if I point out a magnificent sunset sky, I'm told that the colour of Krishna's robe is more glorious. I try to smell a flower but I'm stopped as it hasn't yet been offered to Krishna. There they were in a mini-paradise, Hawaii, and couldn't even enjoy it. The air was positively perfumed and soft and warm. The sun was a huge orb and everywhere grew lush tropical plants, flowers, and fruits. They'll never convince me that I'm in misery.

They must have thought me an awful agent of evil and seduction, judging from the things they corrected me on. One poor guy was caught talking to me. That occasioned two lectures, as the men in saffron aren't allowed to talk to women. I wore my sari too short (I was afraid it would fall off so I rolled it in well). I shouldn't have let the veil fall off my head while I scrubbed the pots. I was told not to smile when talking to the men! That was modified to an intriguing request not to smile "that way." The funniest of all was when we were sitting down in the temple and I was told to cover my feet. Can you imagine my club feet being so provocative as to cause a devotee one uneasy thought?

My sense of humour became strained, though, when they started the line that women were of a lower order than men. Women should be married or they were like lost sheep, unable to fend for themselves. I had a retort or two for that. Yet they were lovely people and kind and good, if a little misguided. And they certainly helped me when I needed it. What was really amusing was dancing out in the streets with them. The reactions were hilarious.

But I got away.

I had been thinking of changing my ticket to Japan and spending time on one of the remoter islands, but when I got to the airport I couldn't be bothered with the hassle. So on I got and a stroke of luck that was, too. When I landed in Tokyo, on an off-chance I tried the number of a friend of a friend from Boston. It was one of those dodgy numbers with a question mark and a smudge. I couldn't believe it when a friendly American voice answered at the other end. She was leaving for the States that afternoon so said I could sleep in her place until Friday when the girl downstairs is leaving and I can have her place until January! Well, I could hardly believe it. If I'd arrived any sooner, there wouldn't have been room at her place. Any later, and I would have missed her.

Her place really is tiny. She shares with another very nice American. It's a doll's house, a two-room affair. The sitting-room furniture gets moved at night for the mattresses to be pulled out. Most Japanese really have no room to entertain. The table is interesting. It's about a foot-and-a-half off the ground but has a quilt attached all around with a heater underneath, so your legs keep cozy. And they really do have those Japanese baths; I'm just over a long, luxurious soak.

Yesterday I went walking around Tokyo for about eight hours. At first I was horrified by what I saw. The day was overcast and grey, the air smoggy and raw. I started in the business district. Seas of people in gray and navy surged around me like so many uniformed army ants. Their faces were expressionless, seemingly choked by their tight, skinny ties. The city, gutted during the war, was modern and bleak; the only relief from the gray was the assault of neon. In my best Japanese accent I could only think "Yuck!" I contemplated a speedy packing and exit.

Then, fortunately, I meandered into neighborhoods where

rigor mortis had not set in and people were smiling. I had fun going through streets festooned with paper lanterns and streamers, listening, smelling, and watching. It's funny trying to get anyplace. I sympathize with illiterates because you can't even read street signs. It becomes a treasure hunt of clues wrestled from waving arms and broken English. I'm already learning a lot. The girl I'm staying with has been here a year and a half and is giving me loads of insights. She's doing anthropological work here and has a ton of books on Japan and the Japanese that I'm looking forward to delving into. At the weekend we're going to another town filled with temples and more traditional buildings. It should be fun. She's great and is certainly making things a lot more pleasant for me. . . .

Love, Maura

PART I

Arrival

WEDNESDAY, NOVEMBER 18, 1979

I phone Toshoji Temple. Am met at temple by Tessai-san. He guides me through mounds of mandarin oranges, under the paper lanterns, past the vendor plying sweet potatoes. He says, "You came at a good time—tea time." There are four monks like little boys, laughing, innocent, delighted to see me. I meet the master, Go Roshi. When I was told that I could stay there, I felt as if I had come home, very settled and bursting with happiness. There are no other foreigners yet.

THURSDAY

I see Ueno Park and great museum. Rodin's *Thinker* sits there looking at a bed of cabbage. I have a job interview. They want to hire me.

FRIDAY

I go to Roppongi. Disappointing. I go for a second job interview. The eejit blathers for three hours on nothing. He just wants cute young Caucasians—the other three candidates are better qualified than I but I'm offered the job. I turn it down.

SATURDAY

I go to the temple. The master can't speak English. They give me my room, four tatami mats wide. There's a little desk, cushion and mattress. We go upstairs to chant. The statues look pagan. I've no idea what I'm getting into. Dinner is disastrous. We kneel around benches. There is a precise way to do everything, a million bows. Silence. The damn egg roll is so big and greasy that I can't pick it up. I'm behind the others, gobbling, trying to catch up. The voice of the master shatters the silence. "You eat slowly." I don't know if it's a comment or a command. I take it as the latter and relax and am grateful that the one thing he said was so right.

SUNDAY

They told me they didn't begin until six on Sundays but they'd already started when I arrived at six. I didn't know what to do. I knelt in the darkness outside Go Roshi's door. As he comes out he smiles and beckons me into the hall. After breakfast, he asks me if I've completed university and how did I know of the temple. He asks me if I'm willing to shave my head, and to beg *[takuhatsu]*. I say okay. He jumps up and springs from the room. I thought he'd gone for the razor but comes back with robes. I model them and everyone laughs with child-like delight. Tomorrow will be my ceremony. I'll get my new name.

I'm late again. I understand nothing, can only watch. I watch as the sun's broad band creeps slowly across the black, glinting on the ivory, catching each monk, one by one. Taro is always at peace. Tenno won't smile. Takeo holds his stomach, tears pricking his eyes.

We do more cleaning. It seems interminable. I sweep outdoors. My bare feet, pink from cold, look wrong peeping from the wooden sandals. I feel wrong behind the whisking bamboo twigs. I cannot understand or be understood.

The afternoon is better. We chat and laugh a bit. They confer for the right word, tell me they are glad I'm here. I love them.

MONDAY

My ceremony. I am named Soshin. I like it. It rhymes with Oisin, a name that has always intrigued me. The others had been given names like 'iron wolf' or 'iron ship,' so I was surprised at how beautiful my name was. It was variously translated as 'great enlightenment,' 'simple mind' or 'warm/open/frank heart.' I'll gladly take any version. I'm to go to Morioka in January to beg. They keep teasing that I'll be famous on T.V. I really enjoyed sawing wood. The monks are not at all sexist. I'm totally "one of the lads" in dress, behavior and treatment. I'd love to be as peaceful and vibrant as Go Roshi. I do wish I could understand him.

TUESDAY

My mind wanders so when I do *zazen [sitting meditation]*. A *gaijin [foreigner]* came, named Frederick. He's been travelling around the world but is still very German. At first I really wanted him to stay but then I realized that I am happier surrounded by only these wonderful Japanese. They are good and pure and simple. Eshin's gentle child's face is so unspoiled, totally without guile. He's loading me with lessons. I hope he tires a bit. Frederick made me glad I wasn't on the outside—there's so much distracting nervousness there.

But I was cold. Bare feet on bare boards. The wind rises between the cracks, and it will get worse. For a little while, trying to be with the cold, I enjoyed it, a nice skin-tensing sensation. Brisk. But, oh my feet!

WEDNESDAY

I finally had a really good meditation. For a few moments my mind stopped its incessant chattering and I was down very deep.

In the morning I felt restless with thoughts of how long I should stay, should I go elsewhere, will I be very old before going back to my own world? In the evening there is meditation and service. I feel very high. We had a banquet afterwards, with sake to drink. I look at these men, laughing, enjoying, knowing. Like the old men in pubs at home, they drink through the grey curls of smoke. They are simple men, kneeling long hours on a cushion, leading spartan lives, but they are no Himalayan hermits. They drink and revel. It would be a good and wonderful thing to grow old like these men.

An ancient man, a great master, comes to pay his respects to Go Roshi. Two women help him hobble up the steps. I gasp in awe and reverence, "He's beautiful." Tetsuro repeats my exclamation and another visiting senior motions for me to follow. We sit, the six of us, in Go Roshi's snug reception room. I feel so privileged. I can't understand a word. The others serve us. I can only watch this man, the power, wisdom and dignity he exudes.

Jiko gives me a drawing of a gold-coloured harp being strummed by a ringleted maiden in an evening gown. "That's you," he says. I'm touched. His name means "sunny." He's always trying out awkward English idioms, like "It's all Greek to me." His face crinkles when he smiles, a Peter Pan. He spends long hours copying chants into *romaji [English characters]* for me.

At the service I feel very high, can't stop smiling. At tea-time the Zen Society gathers and I'm briefly questioned about my intentions.

Jiko tells me I'm to be Go Roshi's jewel. I'm elated. About one meditation a day seems to be a good one.

Today I had my first real *dokusan [interview with Roshi about one's practice]*. (I went before but had no interpreter). Go Roshi gave me the koan of *mu.* * Nothingness. Only mu. I become filled with mu.

[*A koan is a challenging bit of narrative that points to ulti-

mate truth. Many koans have been handed down from teachers in early Chinese Zen Buddhist periods, but all masters in all ages find material at hand for teaching.]

The interpreter and Tetsuro call me to their room. They have both attained enlightenment. They question me about my motives and knowledge. All the time my pulse beats "nothingness, nothingness." Poems have come to me between the beats of mu.

Cathy-san was enlightened in three years, one priest in a year. I need not wait for old age, just follow Go Roshi. I have total faith in him. He can see inside me. He has the strength to kill my ego so that I can be free. "Without fail," he says, "you will attain enlightenment." I can scarcely contain myself. "Nothingness, nothingness." It's like a jungle drum beating through my veins, but I must fight for it. I sleep in a frenzy. I keep awakening hearing "Nothingness, nothingness."

SATURDAY

I work to mu. I hate the interruption of talking because slowly through the day and its idle chatter, nothingness slips. I meditate three times. My body. Inside and all around is nothing. No thing. No separation. A geyser in a lake appears to be a separate thing but is the lake. In the morning there is question-time. I ask Go Roshi the meaning of enlightenment. He strikes me. Not hard. When you are hit, you feel pain.

SUNDAY

Ice cubes in a glass seem separate, have form. The sun shines; where have they gone? Nothing has been taken away. Their separateness is only form and only apparent, a temporary, illusionary state. Plants have consciousness. If there is reincarnation, our consciousness is different; is that of a plant, for instance and not a man trapped in a plant's shape. Our present body does not continue. Our consciousness according to theory would be different, i.e., that of a plant. Thus there is nothing left of the ice cube. We are all nothingness.

ANOTHER WEEK

I told Takeo-san my answer. He said I was enlightened. Wonderful!

Jiko and I went to the English bookstore. I couldn't contain my joy, looking at the dead people, thinking of nothingness.

I went to dok'san. I was determined not to be tricked into using words. Words give form, apparent substance, to nothingness. Roshi asked me what was mu. I said "nothingness." He hit me. What do I feel? I was about to say pain but due to my resolution to avoid words, I said "nothingness." "Continue," he said. I had reached my answer through logic. He was right. Think only of mu, nothing else. Don't study Japanese or sit in the corridor—only mu.

At the English bookstore, all the conflicting theories of Zen and schools had confused and upset me. I bought a book I already had but then refused to read it. Words. I want to know from inside.

The days went on, full of mu. I avoided the others' company, stopped laughing and only thought of mu. At times it drove me crazy—mu, mu, rattling in my brain, not allowed to think of anything else. I jump up and throw it out, annoyed. Other times I go down, down, down with it, down beneath words where my breath is gentle. Like looking up through the lake and the surface is a sentence and I'm below. Gentle at times. Quiet. A little smile slipping across my face. Sometimes I sit an hour and a half before there's five minutes of calm. At times I'm so happy, other times so vexed with my trivial mind.

SUNDAY EVENING

Takeo suggested how I should breathe. I tried and gradually got more and more excited. Mu rose vibrating up my spine, exploded in my head. Everything was simple. I was laughing. Mu was only mu. I felt ecstatic, couldn't contain my joy. I ran out of the hall, kissed the trees, stood in the garden and was the garden, really was it. All through dinner I beamed. Jiko kept staring. The others had described enlightenment. This was so much stronger. I didn't meditate that night, only lay wrapped snug in bed, listening to the rain.

Dear Family,

. . . *my heart will be with you so think of me at Christmas. There'll be no plum pudding here. Bean cakes are nice, though.*

I was settling in nicely to Tokyo life, met a few people and had loads of work opportunities. But I realized I was only meeting gaijin and all the foreigners form a little clique with an occasional Japanese girlfriend or boyfriend. I was speaking no Japanese and wasn't attracted by the culture, so I've taken a leap into real Japan, and ancient Japan at that! I'm living at Toshoji temple and get room and board in exchange for some cleaning every day, and I'm learning zazen. I'm the only woman and only foreigner studying here.

When I arrived at the Togoshi Koen station, I phoned the temple, and they said someone would come down to meet me. I stood up straight, expecting to be greeted by some quiet, dignified old abbot. Next thing, I jump backwards as a bicycle hurtles at me. Billows of black leap and land at my feet as Tetsuro-san straightens his glasses, catches his breath, and welcomes me. At the temple, it's tea-time, and the monks, sitting on the floor, are laughing and smoking and not looking at all austere. They all try out their high-school English and laugh even more. They're lovely, like great big kids, full of fun. I've yet to see one even vaguely vexed. They all

23

chipped together and bought a linguaphone set so that they could talk to me better. So I keep getting "Would you like another glass of soda?" or "Take these suitcases to our room, please."

Each day starts at five o'clock. I wash my face by the light of the moon. I have my own room with four tatami mats and my own little outhouse. The food is good. Our staples are rice and seaweed, but the cook is really talented. Monastery life is certainly a change. I've never done so much bowing in my life. There's a very exact protocol, especially during meals, of bowing and joining hands as if in prayer. They must think I'm very polite because now I just bow at every pause. That way I figure I'm covered.

At times I feel like a cow in labour. You see, my koan is mu, and I'm supposed to bellow this (discreetly, where necessary) at every available opportunity. I scared the wits out of the poor cook, who thought the noise was her cat being brutalized.

So I'm happy, healthy, and out of mischief. Imagine, me in bed by nine every night! And cleaning every day. That's not as bad as I feared. I even clean voluntarily. Can you believe that? They have a wonderful cleaning agent here. We use it on floors, sinks, windows, metal, you name it. Elbow grease. That's it. Not even mops. Everything is done with rags and water.

The place is totally non-sexist. I half expected to be pointed towards the kitchen, but I saw wood and move furniture with the best of them. And no condescending "Didn't she do well?" It's just taken for granted. I'm totally "one of the lads," except I'm not bald. Next month we go up to the north of Japan, to Iwate Prefecture, to do begging. That should be an experience, begging in the snow. They say it's very beautiful there. I'm looking forward to seeing some countryside . . .

Love, M.

MONDAY MORNING

Christmas Eve: I go to dokusan. "How have you apprehended mu?" Mu is mu. I'm smiling, happy, not at all nervous, still elated. "Continue!" The bell goes ting-a-ding-ding. I'm dismissed.

I felt crushed. He didn't know. Didn't he know? How could he know? But I knew. Damn. It was Christmas Eve. I was cold, and sick of *soji [cleaning]*, afraid that Tenno thought I wasn't doing enough, so from guilt I was working more. Hating the guilt. Thinking of home and family and how long I'd be stuck doing stupid, menial cleaning, and with no enlightenment.

Tears prick my eyes. Juro and Eshin, like mother hens, tend me. I sit in Eshin's tiny, dark, freezing hole, wrapped tight in his wool kimono, listening to music. I try to really listen, to stop words. I don't do any soji and wonder what Tenno thinks.

Roshi buys a Christmas cake, the cook buys champagne, and they give me a party. Five monks huddled around wooden benches. When we sing we see our breath. The green plastic holly and frosting tree look odd on the strawberry cream cake. They light the candles. Don't all western cakes have candles? I wait for them to burn down. They toast me and cheer me. Jiko writes out "The Song of Wandering Aengus" on a subway map. It's not Christmas, but it's the Christmas spirit. They gave me a real lift.

Christmas day, like any other day. Even the post office is open. I decide monastery life is not for me. I love life too much to lock myself away. Maybe six months, a good chance to work on myself. It seems my experience of "enlightenment" was as good as Tetsuro's yet Roshi does not accept it. I remember the book says that *Rinzai* and *Soto [sects of Zen Buddhism]* both produce the same effect, so I decide to hell with koans. I'll work on breathing, mental silence, and really being here now. I felt much better. Tetsuro has said several times how hard I work. It's not so, but it relieves my nagging guilt. Zen is very important to me. I think I'll leave by summer but continue to study Zen when I get to Paris.

These men are wonderful. They show me such genuine warmth and love that I'm thriving. At first I took Go Roshi at his word and thought only mu. I wouldn't talk to anyone, dampened myself down. I felt I was going mad. The only variation from day to day was what was on the blue saucer for dinner. Now I'm not so extreme, but maybe it's necessary to go a little crazy to break the ego. Or maybe that's "Zen sickness."

It feels funny to be in my long black robes, darting through the traffic on a sunny bicycle day or waltzing with Jiko in a department store.

Was so still I could feel my heart beat and it was the clock ticking on the wall.

I make it. Making consists of it and me. It and me are one in making.

I tried an experiment to silence my internal chatter, made the running commentary relevant. There is blue, there is smoking, there is sweeping, swish, swish. It made things much richer.

Roshi gave me more clothes. He said my heart was pure. I gave everyone little New Year presents. After dinner, in English, Roshi spoke into the silence. "Very good present, thank you." He bows deeply. I laugh deeply.

New Year's Eve party: These little monks know how to have fun. Here am I, my friends all monks—it seems strange. I sang "Auld Lang Syne." It's the first time I've sung alone in public and not cared. Little by little I'm gaining understanding, though my meditations have been very shallow.

I want to be a Zen master.

PART II

Takuhatsu
(begging)
1980

Funny about my age. Go Roshi's son thought I was thirty. I looked in the mirror and I looked thirty. When I came to here, to *Kannonji [a country temple in Iwate Prefecture, owned by the roshi]*, they say I look a teenager. I look in the mirror and I look like a teenager.

Sometimes mu is so beautiful. Kneeling on the bare boards, by the warmth of the wood stove, the day is a grey, snowy twilight. I'm mixing the soup around and around, brown into a foam, around and around. Breathing deeply and softly, a mu, I feel peace.

Five in the morning zazen. *Sutras [chanting]*, and our breath puffs steam engine billows of icy vapour. I look at these men, their hard, kind faces, and I love them. I then look at the old woman, bent double, who for the past ten years (since she gave the land on which Kannonji was built) has hobbled over to the temple every morning for sutra. A bare silhouette in the pre-dawn light, bent over her cane she shuffles through the snow. And before breakfast we are out shovelling the virgin white, and I don't even mind. Rice and soup, plain and hearty.

Takuhatsu, layer upon layer of clothes, sometimes ten, with our begging bowls and bells we walk slowly through the streets of Morioka, through the snow and sleet, in straw sandals, bells ringing, chanting. The little old women slide open the panel on their doors, drop a coin in a bowl and stand, with bent head and long apron, waiting for a monk's blessing. Sometimes they gasp in surprise when they see me—a woman, a gaijin. When I walk, just walk, chanting, not wondering what time it is or watching the doors, I am very happy.

Riko-san is very hard and very good, a man of precious metal. He walks through the snowstorms to get me warm clothes. He teaches me in simple broken English about Buddhism. He is simple and pure and has no doubts. So too is his wife. I love her. A temple woman asked in wonder whether I was a boy or a girl, then brought her child to kneel before me and kept taking my hands to kiss them. I wonder what she was saying.

There's been much fuss since I was interviewed on TV and in the newspaper. Now people point to me, want to put their offerings in my bowl, children follow me on the street. In jest, Taro-san calls me a goddess, Buddha of the caravan. Silly, because the fuss is on account of my being foreign and female.

The devout women of Morioka invite us to lunches. Oh, such food! They never eat with us—probably couldn't afford to—but reverently wait outside the room. With tears in their eyes they thank us for the privilege of serving us. I watch them on their knees bowing and feel weird to be in this role, especially in another culture from my own. At one luncheon it was decided that I had a Japanese face. Of course my face is as Irish as turf but it's all part of their acceptance of me. Several people have said that I don't seem Western.

When I was in South America I didn't feel estranged either; they said I seemed Latin. Quién sabe?

The woman in the fish shop served us hot *sake* and rice. It's warming, after hours in the snow. All around lie the bodies of fish, bodies heaped on bodies, with gaping eyes and mouths. I no longer want to eat fish. I wouldn't catch one myself. Shellfish and eggs I can handle. But then I eat fish for lunch because I eat what's given me.

January 13, 1980

Dear Family,

Happy birthday to my favorite brother in this whole world. Wish I could be with you. You've gone and grown up behind my back. Hope you like school and you're not showing off too much with all A's. An A- here or there would be good for the other kids. Right?

How was the Christmas for yis? I missed you. Christmas Eve was very cold and glum without a sprig of holly or a sniff of turkey. I was feeling decidedly on the wrong side of the Pacific. Word went around the monastery that I was down in the dumps, and they all rallied round. One monk did my chores for me. Another one

wrapped me in a big woolen coat (it was freezing), popped head-
phones on me and played tapes, his prize being hymns from Notre
Dame. The abbot went out and bought a "Christmas cake," and
the cook bought champagne. They were going to give me a
Christmas party. Well, it was the funniest looking Christmas party
I ever saw. Five monks and the cook huddled in the cold around four
wooden benches. The plastic tree and yule log looked strange sitting
on a "Christmas cake" of whipped cream and fresh strawberries.
They lit birthday candles on the cake. Don't all Western cakes have
candles? But they didn't know what to do with them, so they turned
off the lights and patiently waited for the candles to melt down.
Then they played "Silent Night" in Japanese and took turns
singing English songs. Then Tetsuro-san leaps to his feet in full
monk's regalia, hips swinging, and in choppy Japanese accent he
does his rendition of Elvis Presley. Then there was "Home, home on
the lange." Great cheer all around, though you could see everyone's
breath as each sang his song. The party ended at 8:00; we all had
to be up at 4:30. It wasn't quite Christmas, but it was certainly the
Christmas spirit.

  All the while there was the build-up to going begging this
month. A couple of days before we were to leave for the north, one of
the monks came to my room with an armful of bandages.

  I asked what they were for. "Your wounds," he replied
solemnly. We both consulted our dictionaries to make sure bandages

and wounds were the right words. They were. I closed the door and wondered just what I'd let myself in for this time. I felt as if I was going off to war.

I've hit the news again. Aren't you glad it's not a demonstration this time? Everyone was amazed at a girl and a foreigner going begging. It looks hard, walking for hours through the snow in straw sandals (with socks), chanting and ringing a bell. "Severe training for a boy," they say, "but for a girl?" and their slanted eyes widen. So they interviewed me on TV; then the newspaper for this prefecture came around. I don't know what they wrote. The reporter couldn't speak English, so one of the monks told him all about me. Suddenly I had a public. People in buses would wave and point; children followed me in the street; people chased me to put money in my bowl. Today the newspaper came round again. There was such a response that they want another article.

It's funny, the begging isn't bad at all. I wear literally ten layers of clothes and once the fingers and toes are numb, you don't feel a thing. It's nice walking through the streets singing at the top of your lungs. It's like going Christmas caroling every day. Then the little wooden door rattles and slides across, and an old woman, bent over, clutching her shawl, shuffles in the snow to drop whatever she can in your bowl, then bends her head reverently waiting for the blessing I can't give.

Most days families from the town invite us to lunch. It's a big occasion for them, and they go all out. We wear our ceremonial dress. They put a feast before us. I'm trying all kinds of Japanese delicacies I could never have afforded otherwise. They're on their knees pouring out their thanks to us again and again for coming to their homes. If you could see the old women with tears rising to their eyes, holding the abbot's gown and thanking him. It's so strange to be in this respected position. I'm not used to it in my own culture, let alone this one. Fellows my own age passing in the street who normally would try to chat me up instead join their hands as if to pray and bow deeply. All the while I'm trying to keep a straight face.

This amulet that I'm enclosing was especially commissioned by the abbot for you. It is a New Year's blessing to bring health and happiness to the home. On the right is our name, on the left is the temple and the monk that wrote it (the same one that did Elvis on Christmas Eve). They say it should be hung in a special place.

When you mentioned coming to Japan, I must say, selfishly, I'd love you to come over; it'd be great to see you, but in fact if you're going to spend the money you'd get better value anywhere else. Prices are ridiculous. $20.00 for a steak, $13.00 for a melon, $1.50 for a cup of coffee . . . it's all true. But then you could eat tofu and mandarins and drink green tea instead. Little was left of old Japan after the war; now it's mostly ugly concrete rabbit warrens, but for me it's grand because I'm living in thirteenth century Japan *and it's fascinating. But I must say, of all the countries I've been to, modern Japan would be low on my list of "must come back to's." However, I'd still like to see ya.*

Love, M.

KANNONJI TEMPLE
FEBRUARY, 1980

It was *daikan [great cold]*. The great, coldest, coldest weeks of the year, coldest prefecture of the country. Go Roshi was delighted that I wasn't used to the cold—better training. I told the temperature by whether the offerings were frozen or not, and often they were. So, wiping a metal cup, the cloth would freeze on. Washing in the morning isn't cracking the skin of ice on the basin but taking a blunt instrument and bashing it. Perhaps the hardest part was not the takuhatsu itself but sutras in the morning.

Up and run to the little wood stove in the kitchen. A few minutes respite from the cold, then into *zendo [meditation hall]*. I was first, sitting alone in the predawn dark. The rustling of the robes to the rhythm of running feet, and the bell rings; wood resounds a dull thud. Slowly incense wafts through the zendo. I am more asleep than awake, struggling to incarnate, meditations usually frazzled. Tekkan-san's cushion is always there, so I wonder if he already sat. Tessai, Tessan and Jiko-san all gurgle, splash, spit toothpaste, then drift in one by one. Tachibana *sensei [teacher]*, the village English teacher, and his ten-year-old son. Could I, can I ever do that, lead a layman's life and still attend to my meditations?

From zendo into *hondo [hall for chanting and teaching]* where it's even colder. Sutra clouds of frozen breath. At the end, if I have the control to touch my baby fingers together for obeisances, then I'm glad the day is so warm. Sutra chanting ends and we scurry, run, laughing in the darkness, dashing towards the warmth of the hearth.

Jiko-san, chafing his hands together "Itai, itai" through the chattering of his teeth; Katsuko-san, round, cuddly dumpling, smiles sympathetically; Tessai announces the temperature. I squat among the sticks, my long robes flowing carelessly across them, huddled over the stove, warming my hands and watching the red flickering in the slit. Hypnotizes. Soji for breakfast. Soji—we run, bare feet seem to stick, slightly frozen, to the tatami. We sweep out the snow where it has drifted in the cracks, laughing all the while, more to keep warm than from amusement.

Breakfast is hearty. I hold high my rice bowl, blue bears dance across it. The kerosene fire glows warmly in its ceramic reflection. The rice steam curls mu and I am at peace and thankful. grateful

38

Crossing through the snow in the dawn twilight, I look at the stars. Some days I'm happy, skipping, tingling, other days muttering, promising myself never again, consoling myself—I love you, Maura, you can do it, Maura; it's only X more days, wanting to linger in bed with a cup of coffee, or just once to sleep later than 4:30. I add a couple of sweaters and a kimono, then carry back my takuhatsu gear to the breakfast room. There, with Tekkan-san, I dress, Katsuko-san puttering around, kindly warming damp socks, straightening a belt or fold. Tekkan-san often seems gruff, "Noooo, this way," pulls, pushes, tightens my clothes, pulls my kimono firmly across my chest, just a straightforward arrangement of clothes. Then a few minutes' space before we have to leave, a quiet time. I sit, trying to be empty, to only sit. Sometimes in simple English with many pauses, Tekkan-san would tell me something about Buddha, about life, or read sutra with me. "You must learn to read Buddhist book," he says.

PART III

Tokyo

Yesterday I bought books. I read about mu, read that mu is not a mantra, don't just repeat mu but struggle with What is mu? I went upstairs to zendo mu. I am mu. I am nothing, nothing, nothingness. I do not exist (though I do). But nothing, absolutely nothing. Something trembled near my eyes. I wept, lay down on the tatami and wept huge, heaving tears. I was nothing, my dreams, my hopes, my conceits were nothing. I cried funeral tears. I was at my own funeral and no one else had come. I was crying and crying and crying and. . . .

Downstairs, it was time to make toast. Tetsuro-san asked what was wrong. I am nothing, and it's very hard and very sad and tears pricked. "Honto? You are near enlightenment. You must go to dokusan." I know I'm not near enlightenment but I would like to go to dokusan. I do mu, a deep total mu. Afterwards my vocal cords hurt. Roshi says keep with mu 'til *sesshin [an intensive week of zazen]* and then I will attain enlightenment. (As for that "will"—try "may.")

After dinner, Roshi says "put an ad in the paper for a new cook." He doesn't like my cooking. The fish was too hard (two weeks old, I scraped off the mold), the salad too hearty. It was true. I wasn't that put out. It was true. Though I liked cooking, wished it had been good. I felt too drained to really react, to be really hurt. After all the tears, I had heard the shock of Tekkan-san's possible dismissal by the people of

Morioka. There seemed to be an enormous web of conflicting saying and thinking. Morioka people had seemed so warm, generous, and appreciative of Tekkan-san, yet the dear little old ladies deftly stabbed him through the heart. Roshi dismisses us; the others say they're always hungry but grumble about too much food. I am tired, little sleep, and I am nothing—exhausted, spent. And Jiko-san says, "You are too simple and too honest." And for that time he is right. I can scarcely even feel bewildered, only wash the dishes and go to bed.

You must struggle with a koan, fight with it and for it. My energy in mu is renewed asking, What is it? Getting up in the morning is one of the hardest things for me. So I will get up even earlier and go to the hondo and sit.

FEBRUARY 22

> *I was not born*
> *will not die*
> *for I am*
> *nothing*
> *but please do not*
> *stand on my*
> *toe.*

If mu is mind, consciousness, it is nothing. I am always changing—not a thing. I am not the same person as ten years ago, or a moment ago, yet I am. But then where is I? A fish has the consciousness of a fish. I have the consciousness of a twentieth-century woman and no one before has had my consciousness. Where is rebirth? Consciousness changes. If reborn as a fish, I am a fish, not Maura, but a fish. Consciousness changes. Action and reaction, like a seal stamped on sand. Nothing is transferred, but the processes continue. Energy cannot be created or destroyed, only transformed. What is dead and what alive? He said, first and last thoughts. Makes sense. Plants and animals think. Has a stone consciousness? Is it conscious? If consciousness is energy, all form is, not has, consciousness. If we all are not have mind . . . huh? . . . what? . . . hmmm. Are things *mu [nothing]* and *u [something]*? Waves on the ocean are separate but the same. When the wave subsides it doesn't disappear, cease to exist, but does. It is no longer the wave but the ocean which is what it was anyway. Isn't that death? And mu is u and Joshu can say the dog has no Buddha nature.

Dinner was almost a fiasco. Jiko-san, at the last moment, added sauce and soothed my laments.

Does the first thought mean the beginning of a new life because thought is separation?

Roshi asked Jiko-san to place the ad [for a new cook]. He keeps changing his mind. He apologized and asked us to cook for a while, saying it's good to have cultivators in *tenzo [kitchen, or cook]*, then changes. Jiko and I were sitting eating the brown rice glue that we have dubbed jiko-mochi and that I love, I saying the only thing I like more than tenzo is the garden. I didn't look forward to the hours of dusting the clean altars I had dusted the day before. Then Tessan-san tells me my new job will be the garden. I can't believe it; I'm overjoyed.

Form is emptiness. It is never the same, always changing, so doesn't exist, is mu; but bang into the wall, of course; and form is form.

My life force is always being passed into new forms. Each cell born in my body contains my life force and each one that dies is dead. Is it so strange that it passes into a new body? Yet there is no "it." Nothing is transferred. It's the same with cells. I'm having a lot of trouble with this death-rebirth business. It's incredible. Cells divide. Then each one knows what to do. All the minute things, another me, all functioning. Miraculous.

The thing to which I am most attached, can least give up, least admit its transience, is myself.

FEBRUARY 25

I get up and go to zendo at 4:00. Not so hard. Sitting alone, trying the new mu that Jiko-san has taught me. It's more open; I prefer it. I raise and put back my head, saying mu. Someone turns off the light and comes into the room. Perhaps even Roshi. In the darkness I make out the pattern of the doors. It's a warm enveloping dark, a womb, dark, shared with I don't know who. It's peaceful and comforting. I will sit every morning in that stillness.

The figure is Tetsuro-san—Iron Wolf, prowling, always a little unsure, a little outside. His kindness and compassion to me have been enormous, an encouraging and humble word whenever I need it. He is soon to become abbot of a new temple and seems to be anxious. Jiko says he's neurotic.

He himself says he imagines people want to get rid of him. He startled me at the sink when he pounced. "Why were you laughing?" About him, he thought. "Joke, joke," he said. Honest in his weaknesses and nightmares. After all his generosity to me, when I had the chance to get him a takuhatsu hat, I did. It cost 10,000 yen but with my takuhatsu money, it wasn't that much, and money is for such things. He said he worried all night, distraught, asking himself why I had given him such a big present. Issh. He's so funny, so childlike, the way he opens his heart. He's poring over the newspaper.

"Aha." Face alight. "Olivia Hussey has married a Japanese."

"Oh, really?" and I add something forgettable about her, not sure of the relevance of the announcement.

"What do you think of international marriages?"

I approved.

"So you would marry a Japanese?"

"I'd need to learn Japanese."

Then he throws himself into excited jabbering with Mio-san, the gist being that I wasn't against marrying a Japanese. I love his innocence.

I was sitting up in zendo, and Jiko's words were in my ears. "When you are your mother, when you are Roshi, then you are enlightened." I didn't see how that was possible. If I wasn't myself, I certainly wasn't them. I kept telling myself: you are everything. Hard to conceive of. Then it hit me how totally arbitrarily we have defined our so-called self. I am my body, thoughts, perceptions, personality. So the thought of my mother is me but my mother is not. The real "I" I've defined as not me, and that which is merely the image and not real I have defined as me. Strange. The spit in my mouth is me. The air in my mouth is not. The food I take in isn't, yet somewhere it passes some vague border and becomes me. I myself was so arbitrarily defined—the thought is me, the spit and food is me, but the painting I produced, spawned from my thought, is not me, the tune humming though my head, me—and if I any way reject that definition of self as non-existent, can't I then redefine myself?

And I began. Each noise, sight, movement was me. I was tremendously excited, quivering, smiling. As if there was a statue, my physical body, with a cloth draped over it, hanging close around my body; it was what I defined as self. Now a tack through the head and cloth, someone is raising it and stretching it; it's still attached to my body but covers more and more, and that is me. How can I die or cease to be? I am eternal; I am process and thing. I am my mother. I am Roshi. I left the hondo, a new I; every noise and sight caught my notice, being incorporated into myself.

We went shopping. I cooked dinner, and soon my self-conception was back to its usual stifling structure. Does Roshi always feel like that? Before I admired him for having stared at his nothingness in its coffin and still being able to laugh. Now it seemed there was much more. Enormous.

After zazen, Roshi said something about *muji [the koan mu]* being everything and about the tenzo people (Jiko and I) working from devotion. So maybe it's not because he hates my cooking that he wants a new kitchen helper.

FEBRUARY 29

My relationship with Jiko has been interesting. I always oscillated between being amused at his childlike pranks and being irritated by his childish demands for notice. Constantly praising himself, yet as quick and enthusiastic in his praise of others. I don't believe he has ever criticized another's character—their habits, yes, but not their character. He often seemed to act uppity with me, correcting me on trivial points, straightening a wrinkle, this way, pushing me. It was annoying in a mild way. So I wondered how he'd get on in the kitchen. I can see how I've changed in my reactions. He often flaps around, does nothing, or fiddles with his dictionary while I do all the work. He asked me to do all the lunches since he "sometimes has business." Rubbish. My first reaction was, Hold on, make sure you're really doing more before you accuse, then point out how much you did, etc. Do the lunch and put up with it. Instead, I said no. If he had business I'd do the lunch and he could do it for me the next day.

I asked which day to put out the bins. "Today," he blithely said. "Where do they go?" Starting to resent. "Over . . ." He began to indicate. Before, I would have taken them off, fumed and forgotten it as unimportant. I ordered, "Come on." Not giving him time to take off his slippers at the door, I gruffly commanded, "Take those." He did, obviously meek and chastened.

In the kitchen I tell him to put things away if I feel put upon. In fact, now I can laughingly give him the towel or just shut up when he goes on and on and on and on, asking me to repeat the pronunciation of some word "merry," "merry," "merry," "merry." So no tension builds up. The moment it rises, it flickers, and so we laugh and joke and love working in tenzo.

He never takes the meals too seriously, which is good for me, though often disaster for the cooking. Every morning he makes mochi—a healthful, gluey combination of *komugi [wheat]*, beans, *gemmai [brown rice]*, peanuts or *goma [sesame]* or whatever comes to hand. We sip tea, eat slowly, and listen to his tiny radio. It's a simple, gentle, very great pleasure. He often adds charming touches, like serving on a special plate or with flowers. He does make me laugh so.

For Roshi's son's birthday party, the 27th, we had to prepare a big, sit-down dinner for fourteen. *Ok'san [Go Roshi's wife]* wanted two kinds of fish and a meat. I decided to positively avoid getting into a flap . . . three gas burners, no oven or even a grill. I had my part all ready by 10 o'clock in the morning of the 27th: chicken, fish, each separately marinated. Twice Jiko's rice came out too soft. I was helping him, so there was still a countdown tension but not bad. My chicken was very cold, being in the fridge, so I put it in the rice steamer and the outside went wet. I nearly died. My crispy delicious chicken. I quickly started re-frying and all went well.

Dinner—even I must admit—was delicious and beautiful. Roshi's son didn't show up. Roshi, from the other end of the table, beaming, said in English "Zank you verly much." He's radiant. "*Do itashimashite*" *[You're welcome]*, I muttered, and all oohed. It was a success. Jiko and I hugged, shook hands, laughed, and after cleaning, sat down with flowers and finished the sake. Bejaysus it was grand.

In the afternoon I had time to spare. Tetsuro-san was cutting Tetsubun-san's hair. I shot some pictures and sat lazily in the sun, half in and half out of the big glass window. Playfully flicking the shears, Tetsuro-san teased, "Now, how about you?" I thought for a few minutes. My hair was growing, looking well, would soon be long enough to part in the middle. I had bought a hairbrush, thinking of getting a mirror. "How about you?" "Okay," I said. The day was warm; my hair was in the way; when would I have the chance to be bald again?

"Honto?" "Ii yo." Tetsuro-san jumped up and jumped down, asked Tetsuban-san, asked Jiko-san, put on his kimono to ask Roshi, then took it off, then put it on and finally shore off my hair.

Surprisingly, it didn't bother me. Of course, with no big mirror I don't see myself. The air and wind feel good on my head. It's a liberating feeling. I remember reading about light affecting some gland corresponding to a third eye in the case of shorn birds. Interesting. The next day it snowed. My bald head was very cold.

After zazen on the 28th, Roshi said it was sad to visit his family. His son took no joy in his birthday. All his family are in education and have no interest in zazen. How sad for him and sad for them. The opportunity they have let slip. I admire his emotional openness with us.

I feel very privileged to be at Toshoji. Roshi is a very great teacher and example. People think the life is hard, but I am grateful. Imagine, all my bodily needs taken care of and that which I most want to do—a very self-oriented thing—is not only tolerated but encouraged. Not a care in the world, no worries or regrets, only this enormous opportunity.

I wonder if every living thing doesn't have compassion—Buddha nature. All life has/is (not sure which) consciousness. Plants faint when an egg or shrimp is killed. Is this not compassion at its most basic? It will be argued that many people are bad. I have yet to meet the person whom I could point to and say "he has no compassion." Reflecting on all the goodness shown to me on my travels, I can only be humble, goodness far exceeding what I am big enough to repay.

These days I feel very conscious of life. Before, I didn't like eating meat because it was so toxic and I found rather insipid the sentimentality of "poor little things." Now it really saddens me to consume flesh, to see slaughter displayed in the supermarket. "Lashai, Lashai, Lashais," welcome. I feel remorse because of the extra wooden match I use, and though I must serve meat and fish to the others, I wonder where to determine my complicity in the crime. I would not by choice serve meat, but each time that I serve it instead of something else (as I must), must I assume this guilt?

MARCH 1

There was no answer to the ad for a new cook. Yesterday Roshi asked us if we would continue cooking. He said at first he thought we were trying to kill him, hard rice and dinner that smelled like medicine. I have to laugh; I love his frankness, but now he says everything is delicious. He thought we would soon tire of the kitchen, but we are in high spirits, and the kitchen is always clean. Jiko said that of course I would rather do the garden, but it's okay. It's still cold for the garden.

This morning, meditating, I couldn't still my mind for a moment. I kept thinking of different things to cook, etc. Was annoyed with myself. After morning sutra we had the ceremony where each person roars a question and Roshi answers. Tetsuro-san told me to go up.

"I don't know what to say," I whispered, flustered.

"Sit there," he said. So I thought I didn't have to ask a question.

Then Roshi calls, "Soshin-san."

I go up and wait for Tetsuro-san to tell me the Japanese I must say. Nothing. I look at him imploringly. "What do I say?"

"Ask your question." So I ask but my voice is small because of the awe and confusion I feel. "What is Buddha?"

I have so many questions. He waits a long time. I cannot understand the answer. Afterwards Tetsuro-san says, "Roshi said, 'You are silent, but your mind is like thunder.'"

I feel crushed. He's saying my mind is a storm; I have no peace. I think of that morning's scattered meditation, how hard it often is to keep my mind on things. He knows I'm so far from enlightenment, it seems like no use—I'll never calm my mind. I ask Jiko what he meant. "Only an allusion to the weather; never mind." I go again to Tetsuro-san. He says it is a common Zen phrase, no bad meaning, comes from a Chinese poem and is like saying, "the old man is silent but his life is etched in his face." I'm slightly consoled.

Chosan [morning tea at which Roshi discusses important things]. Roshi has been appointed one of the top teachers in Japan. How could I have been so lucky to stumble upon his temple, decide to stay (under the illusion he spoke English), be accepted, and have to pay nothing?

Roshi said something about when I was silent this morning. The other Roshi who came to announce Ban Roshi's promotion said he admired me coming as a foreigner and doing Zen seriously, that I was simple in my confusion. Jiko fumbles to translate, and Roshi cuts in, saying in English, laughing, "You are wonderful, number one."

Yesterday I went to enquire about my visa with Tetsuro-san. Watching all the people on the train, they seem lifeless; even Tetsuro-san was slumped into customary subway slumber. People's eyes are blank, or drifting across each other, creating a distance within the crowd by avoiding eye contact. I, too, am good at this. I try to catch the people's staring eyes so I can shatter the game with a smile. No use. They won't let our eyes meet or acknowledge the obvious that we are both there, three hours on the subways. The only one who would communicate with my eyes was a mentally retarded girl on a Saturday group outing. And she's the one defined as out of touch with reality.

Two little boys and their father boarded. They quivered with life and excitement, chattering, laughing, playing, looking at everything with wonder, yo-yos, and curiosity, eyes sparkling. How is it killed, I wondered. They asked their father a question. He ignored them. Another question, a mumbled response as he stares vacantly into space. That is how the crime takes place. And he is a good father; he takes the kids out on Saturdays. Watching them, I want to play— to play tip and tig, hide and seek, pirates, house, red rover, to pretend. Mothers are so annoyed when children return late for tea. How wonderful to be so engrossed, to so enjoy what one is doing that one loses all conception of time. If only mothers could rejoice.

Sunset was beautiful.

This morning Mt. Fuji was clear between the smoke stacks and the railroad tracks. 5:00 a.m. Go Roshi leaves for Iwate. I hope he brings back good news of Tekkan-san.

Everything that happens to me is a mixture of the circumstance and my reaction to it. Nothing can touch me purely without my filtering it, even if the mind is empty. By allowing everything in, I have affected the circumstance. The I-filter is constantly changed, too, by circumstance. "Karma means everything that happens, we directly or indirectly, partly or entirely, set in motion." At least insofar as the circumstance includes the I-filter, this is true, but possibly even the strong case that the quote suggests. You and outside you are not separate. If someone steals all my possessions and I am upset, I say something bad has happened to me. If I do not care, nothing bad has happened, yet it is the same external circumstance.

MARCH 3

Yesterday, sitting, the same question ricocheted round and round my mind. How are we all one? We're all made of the same stuff but that doesn't make us one. Kapleau says Mary hurt in Detroit, Joe feels in Rochester. But I don't. At least not consciously. Then I thought of the plants mourning the egg, excited when many miles away his owner came. I thought of how at Grandpa's death, Aunt Elaine got up in the wee hours of the morning, put on her coat, stumbled through the blizzard, and was with him when he went. Tears came into my eyes. There is knowing between minds. Perhaps (of course) it is usually inaccessible to consciousness. But that it happens at all, and that it is always present in plants, which don't have as complex a consciousness as we do, would seem to mean something.

In the afternoon I was very aware. Without an effort, I was just doing whatever I was doing, without distraction or forcing. Occasionally the thought would pop into my head "Hey, your mind is still." Then even that vanished. Because I was quiet, I was very surprised when Jiko said, "You are in very high spirits."

Today, business and flighty mind as usual.

MARCH 4

Yesterday I went shopping with Jiko. I bought a flash and tripod. I find myself slightly annoyed by his dilly-dallying, pulling and tugging at me, poking me to look at this and that. "*Ii ne, ii, ii*" *[That's good, isn't it? Good! Good!]*, on and on even after I answer him. I know we won't have time to do everything, and of course we don't. But I'm more annoyed with myself for lacking a spontaneity. Everything he shows me is marvelous, and we can do the other things another day. We did what was most important, the flash, and saw wonders. I feel perhaps am being too hard, asking him not to repeat, not to poke me. (Rather, I tell him it's okay for him to repeat but I won't always answer.) When I tell him that and he looks at me with the same expression and intonation as usual "*ii*" or "*oishii*" [tasty] and I don't answer or only say "mm," he persists and persists. He nags until I answer not just "ii" or "ishii," but "ii yo!" or "oishii yo!" and I wonder if he is dense or trying to annoy. I really don't think he has the meanness in him for the latter but hate to conclude the former. And of course it's equally my reaction. If I were more totally immediate, the repetition would not be annoying because each time would be as the first.

Last night I borrowed without permission one of Roshi's books. I felt very guilty and stayed up too late reading. I'm tired and grumpy this morning. Jiko tells me to come over at 9:00 for *omochi* [rice cakes]. I'm starving. He fiddles around for an hour and a half with the windows wide open, taking pictures and dropping my batteries. Then I'm freezing and starving. I'm disgruntled and more annoyed with myself than with him. Why should a change from what I had expected be annoying? I decide I'd better rest. The morning is gone.

Back to the kitchen to make lunch. No Jiko. The kitchen's a mess, his breakfast dishes still sitting, ten o'clock tea dishes still sitting. Of course, I had also left the latter. I'd hoped he'd put away the breakfast dishes, since he'd done nothing else afterwards. I can't say I do more work, because he spends more time in the kitchen, so though my work time there is more industrious, I have more free time. I'm making lunch. Still no sign of him. Well, the only help he is is to get out a few chopsticks. He had asked me to do lunches, and I virtually do, and don't mind as it's easy. But I didn't want him to take it for granted. I don't really feel over-worked, as there isn't that much to do and usually it was a one-person job. I do what's necessary, and if I feel resentful, I give Jiko a dish towel, usually with a laugh. I'm annoyed at myself for being so petty and decide I'm really tired and should sleep more.

Jiko comes in, all apologies. He'd been in a sound sleep. So he wasn't taking me for granted; it was an accident. I felt much better. Of course it was okay. He started going on and on about how I did much more work—still just fiddling with his dictionary while I worked. I handed him a tea towel and said it was okay. We're a team. There's no need to make comparisons, more or less work; we'll just each do our best. I'm glad the sentiment came from him, and really I don't mind doing more, so long as he does something. I also think he finally got it about the repetitions. We'll see. It is much better for me to be working with Jiko-san than with someone who never annoys me.

Reading that book, I feel so far from enlightenment. Not that it's so important for right now, but I'm on such a gross and sloppy level. Why can I not feel the unity of all?

MARCH 5

Why can I not still my mind? Last night's and this morning's meditations were so scattered.

The day before yesterday some psychologists came to test our skin potential, resistance, and breathing during meditation. Jiko was first. He came downstairs and told me how twice during meditation he had left his body and the researchers will be very surprised. I thought about my own meditations, how they are often so sloppy. In the afternoon I went up. A wire from my ear, two around my waist and five in my left arm. I really felt like a laboratory rat. I might have been peevish (as I was a bit for the news interviewer), this "probing a freak" bit, but the researcher does zazen himself so I wanted to cooperate. My meditation was deep. I was one with everyone and everything, including them. I felt strong love for them. At one stage I was their machine, and its rotations were my heartbeat. At the beginning and end we just sat naturally. They rechecked the apparatus and kept telling me to just be at ease. I thought I must be nervous and it was showing up.

At the end they came over, extremely excited, "*Subarashii, subarashii [splendid, splendid]*." "This is very rare data," they said. "We have tested many monks, 40-60, but this is very rare. . . . Your natural state is thirteen breaths a minute and in meditation three or four a minute; normally a good meditation is three to five." They want to test me again next week. I was very pleased, and it was hard for me not to tell the others everything they said, but I don't want the thing to seem competitive. I needed encouragement and it came. However, the things they are measuring are only by-products; they have nothing to do with my understanding, and it is this that I want.

I have been meditating now consistently for three months. (They couldn't believe that—thought it must be a year and three months.) I can perceive subtle changes. My posture is different, composure better. I'm more quiet. I remember finding Sean's silences unbearable and needed constant chatter and once had to stop myself from begging him to talk about just anything. I'm no longer compulsive in eating and drinking. If I do something, I like to do it properly, and I care less about others' opinions of me. I can even serve a bad dinner, feel sorry that it was bad, but not be upset to the core and watching each expression. I'm much better disciplined, but I don't know how permanent any of these changes are. So I am a bit afraid to go back to the "real world."

Mum sent a letter saying she was sad I had given up the idea of a Ph.D. at the Sorbonne (which of course I haven't) and appealing to me to help her sell her Dublin house in the summer. But I am finally doing what I have wanted and needed to do all my life and am afraid to break. I consider Buddhism my "religion," if it can be called that. On the other hand, I do want to continue with my outside life at some stage and finish the koans. So maybe I should find a suitable temple and get on with it, as I'll have to break from here sooner or later. I love, respect, and trust Roshi completely, yet I should not be attached even to him.

TOSHOJI, TOKYO
MARCH, 1980

Dear Mum,

Many thanks for the parcel. Did you realize you had two of my favorite songs on the tape, in addition to "Raglan Road?" I don't know what made you think I'd given up the idea of a Ph.D. at the Sorbonne. For the first time since I left Trinity, I feel I'm making real progress on a would-be original thesis. Things are really clicking, and I'm writing notes all the time. As you know, I got very interested in theories of language, ideology, and the formation of the subject, especially Lacan's work. He is, of course, in Paris. Now learning my first non-western language and being immersed in oriental philosophy, many things are falling into place. As I'm sure you're aware, Zen has very different notions of the subject than ours, and grammatically the language is built to facilitate this. Or was it the other way around? Interestingly, most grammar books, in translating, do not make a direct translation, making the different concepts involved more obvious. But they also translate conceptually, so that the Westerner hears the Japanese phrase but can still think it in his own terms. Luckily, I have found an excellent book written by linguists from Yale that's extremely helpful. My ideas so far stem from Lacan's theories, but I've never seen them applied in such a case. In fact, I can think of a better way of confirming some of his speculations. It's very exciting but difficult, as I can only proceed at the pace at which I'm learning Japanese. I also need to study Shinto and probably linguistic changes that occurred with the impor-tation of much of the Chinese written language, with Buddhism itself, and at the ideological level, with the attempt to introduce the Chinese political system, and how was all this reconciled with the emperor's god status—all of which occurred at about the same time. This is a huge subject, and it's the linguistic end that is most inter-esting and most original.

But it involves a load of work. I have to learn two more Japanese scripts, one of which is non-syllabic. Nonetheless, if I can pull it off it would put me in an important place in my field, though I'm afraid to get my hopes too high.

As I've said to you before, all this meditation has brought me many benefits, not least of which is much greater concentration and self-discipline. I really don't know if I would have been able to undertake a good thesis three months ago. I was so out of the habit of applying myself to anything seriously. Waitressing til three in the morning was not the most conducive thing to academics.

The other day some psychologists from some university came over to do tests on us and psychophysiological changes during zazen. They attached five wires to my arm, hung one from my ear and put on two respiratory monitors. They hadn't told the others anything about the results of their tests, but I resolved to ask them, because I was very curious. But after I finished, they came bounding over, full of non-scientific excitement and saying "wonderful, wonderful" over and over. They said they have tested nearly sixty monks but that my results were extremely rare and apparently I have been having deep meditations that are normally only reached after years of practice. So they want to do a whole bunch more tests on me and are coming back next week. Well, I was very surprised, though I have increasingly noticed changes in myself.

All of which brings me to what is my problem at the moment. This is the first thesis that has really absorbed my interest, that I feel I could put the necessary time and effort into, and that would be worth writing, in that it would be a real contribution. At the same time, I want to keep up my Zen. I was fortunate to end up with a really excellent teacher. He is famous (as are his books) throughout Japan and has just been given the highest recognition there is as a "teacher of teachers." But if I pursue the thesis, it would mean at least another year and a half in Japan. That's a heck of a long time.

The other problem is I don't have the books I need and it would be nearly impossible for you to send them, as I'd have to

search through bookshops, consult bibliographies, and probably be in
touch with Brian Torode and Jim Wickham in Trinity. So I want
your advice, i.e., "Mommy, what should I do?" Please try to be as
objective as possible about it. I imagine your first reaction might
be—two years or two and a half. I suppose I could manage. What
do you think, you having been through the "get back to the books
and really write" bit? But it is a long time.

Love, M.

MARCH 8

Go Roshi came back from Kannonji yesterday; I really love him.

The day after Jiko slept through lunch, I asked him to put away the breakfast dishes, since everything else was done. I came in to find no sign of him. Half-way through lunch and he still hadn't appeared. I thought of someone else's words: "We are one, when a boil appears on your hand, you're not angry at it; you just do something about it." So I did. Jiko was moving rooms when I came in. He, of course, was engrossed in and delighted with the fun of it. I said "Come and help me make lunch." He said, "Oh," surprised.

65

A while later he came in. I said, "Jiko-san, I asked you to put away the dishes. I cleaned everything else. It's not so much to ask." I didn't like to make the comparison. I repeated myself; it often takes a while for things to sink in. Chastened, he did so. That evening he was all "May I help you? What can I do?" Next day he put away without my asking, but the following day he was back to normal. I hate to always prick his balloon. He is quite marvelous—a child's sense of fun, and what child likes to dry dishes? He is eager to cook new concoctions. "Ah, the joy of creation," says he. He goes to infinite trouble arranging glasses of water to play a tune with the radio. He meticulously cuts a piece of potato into a star, selects the right frying pan as a backdrop—the north star against a midnight sky, then pops it into my mouth. He truly has magic in his heart. I feel like Martha with Mary when I ask him to clean. I never thought of myself as a Martha. His strength also is admirable. I don't think I could ever fast for twenty-one days.

At last I am intellectually convinced of the indivisibility and nothingness of everything, but to integrate this into consciousness is so difficult.

Babies are never angry. Unhappy and hungry, of course, but not angry. Anger may be a learned emotion.

MARCH 9

Jiko-san asked Roshi if I should go home, as duty would dictate, or stay. He emphatically said, "Stay." He said, for peace in this world Zen is necessary, and he has an idea for me to start a *dojo [meeting place for Zen practice]* in Ireland. Hmmm. In the far future it's a possibility.

I felt a bit upset because I didn't in my own mind know what to do. Finally a good solution hit me. I'd stay two years with Roshi but go home in July to help Mum move house, see everyone after three years' absence, then come back to Japan. Seems expensive but a good solution. Mom needs help, and I can explain my ideas better in person. Or better yet, perhaps she can see changes in me. I wrote her a letter stressing the academic things I could do here but also explaining my desire to continue to do zazen. I told her how much I loved her and thanked her. I'll wait for a reaction before I mention meeting her in July.

I've been made "altar boy" now. It's more interesting but hard to remember everything.

Yesterday there was a death ceremony. I tried to put all my energy into awakening the dead spirit, and the outpouring was powerful. After the ceremony, Roshi was telling the people the news of Toshoji and praising me. He's very thoughtful.

Jiko-san and I have been having a great deal of telepathy lately. It's almost chilling. I'll think something and he'll say or do it, again and again. He too was amazed and kept saying, "Who are you? Who are you?" He says many praising things, but I'm really not at all extraordinary, and I don't know what to say. I'm trying to avoid making unnecessary distinctions and having to respond to needless praise doesn't help. I was practicing sometimes not using "I," separating myself from my emotions.

Tessan-san started going on about how Jiko and I must eat the same food as everybody else. We weren't eating meat or fish. I feel peeved. Reminding myself that it wasn't really "I" who was peeved helped, but I'm still very much attached to my ego.

I stood by the open window in the warm spring wind, washing noodles. They were wet, soft, moving between my fingers. The moment was eternal.

Jiko-san said I was an excellent Zen *obosan [ordained follower of Buddha]*, and I realized it was the first time I had been called an obosan. It was very pleasing. He said he wondered if I was an incarnation of an old Zen master. He sees good in everyone.

Go Roshi said we must lead simple lives. Apparently he said the researchers were bad because they left on the light when they went away. I hope he didn't really say they were bad—they're forgetful maybe.

MARCH 10

My mind these days is so much calmer, still hardly empty, but stiller. The kitchen is such a pleasure. Two years of daily dusting dustless altars would have been impossible drudgery. Ah, but the tenzo—every day different, a creation. Two years would be not only possible, but wonderful.

Such happiness of late. But there's still attachment.

That's why there's the fear that if I left here the peace might also leave. When even the peace isn't clutched at, then there'll be peace.

MARCH 11

Holding up my soup *chawan [bowl, also soup]*, steam curling, all of us giving thanks, the miracle became apparent, the daily alchemy. This had been life, killed and now made me, made my life. Humble beans and onions passing into me, supporting me, becoming me and I in turn passing into nourishing beans or maybe onions. Endless magical stream, not really of creation and destruction, only a flow.

Funny how in front of seventeen people, most of whom I don't know, I can, as altar boy, make mistakes, be corrected and feel no blush.

The notion of a nation is to a country what ego is to a body.

MARCH 12

Zenkai [also zazenkai; Zen meeting or class]. Up late. Didn't want to get up in the morning. Got up. Yesterday the meditations were terrible, hardly there at all.

This morning at chosan, Go Roshi said the kitchen was the best it's ever been, always clean and good food. He said he left the whole business in our hands. He also said he wants Jiko to ascend to the highest level of the Soto sect. Jiko says he's not interested; as an ordinary man he's more free. I think I am still attached enough to ambition that I would at least be pleased and would not refuse. Or maybe not. Who knows? Today Tekkan-san's destiny is decided. I'd prefer him to stay in Kannonji so that I could spend the summer with himself and Kas'ko-san.

It seems that at zenkai last night, Go Roshi was very critical of Japan, of education, of modern, free-loving women. He said the latter will die (but who won't?). I don't know how faithful the translations are of what he says. I'd rather not think of him as being so all-condemning. Surely all is neither good nor bad. But then, maybe that applies also to Go Roshi. Because I love him so much, I want him to be perfect.

MARCH 13

Tekkan-san came. I was very happy to see him and he the same. He kept shaking my hands and smiling and rubbing my bare head, laughing. I wanted to get him a present to bring to Kas'ko-san, but when I returned he'd already left. He must not have been happy with the results of the talk, for he left hurriedly without a good-bye to anyone. Mio-san chased him on a bike. This morning there was no chosan, so we don't know the results.

I mentioned that I might hitch a ride and catch a boat to Korea. Tetsuro-san's eyes grew round with horror and he told me fantastic stories of gangs with knives, who'd pump me with heroin and force me to do strip shows, or they'd throw my dagger-riddled, bleeding body into the sea. Jiko was not so vivid but insisted I'd need fluent Japanese or I'd get lost. They would never be able to really understand me.

Jiko-san is in many ways wise and a wonder. His koan (very awkwardly translated) means something like "everything is okay." When I told him that this sometimes seemed difficult to reconcile with Go Roshi's *"dame,"* [that's wrong] he said he didn't have that problem. The koan was okay; Roshi's talks were okay; everything was okay. He's no longer bound by the formal, logical requisite of consistency.

At zenkai last night, Roshi talked about mu. How one must be totally involved with it. Dogen sat for one thousand days with mu and ten minutes of only pure mu is a feat for me. Paradoxical, these ancient masters, because their desire is so strong that their ultimate freedom from desire is total. If I could only be so impassioned.

I got a letter from some librarian who had read about me in the paper. He's going to Ireland in May and wanted me to teach him Irish.

MARCH 15

Tekkan-san's fate is still not decided. Tessan-san's pre-priest ceremony was held this morning. He may have to replace Tekkan-san. At the ceremony I messed up my part but strangely didn't feel embarrassed. Nor did I mind shouting out my questions in front of everyone at shosan, though last night at the end of my introduction, I blushed deeply. I was trying to express the gratitude I felt to everyone, but Jiko didn't even try to translate. Translation can be a problem. At this morning's *shosan [questions in front of everyone]* I asked, "What becomes of dead people?" It was translated "Why do people die?" Go Roshi's answer was rendered as: "You study more Buddhism and you will understand that they do not die." He smiled his eyes into my eyes so sweetly, but Ho-san told me that that was an inaccurate translation.

A man came from Kyushu. He sits sure and solid as a mountain. His little son came, too. He sat through meals, squirming, wriggling, slurping, watching with a child's wonder-filled eyes. I loved to see the spontaneity. We "Zenites" seemed self-conscious by comparison, though comparison is not really appropriate. Mio-san corrected him. Each morning of the ten days they stayed, he got up brightly, in little shorts, behind a dim flashlight, bobbing in the dark. Exercises and zazen, he does the lot. He sat last night through all of zenkai. Our eyes caught, and we were shutting and averting eyes like young lovers. He finally giggled, and I tried not to look. Afterwards, I was in the kitchen washing-up and he came in and we laughed and laughed, though we couldn't speak one word to one another. Children are such noble teachers.

MARCH 16

My moods changed so yesterday. Afternoon, lovely zazen in the sunshine. Evening, distracted, unable to focus. I got frustrated; I'm hopeless, useless. I waited up to give Go Roshi a late dinner. He beamed, really seemed to emit light, and I was elated. He said, "*Saiko*" *[The best!]* but Tessan-san was outraged. However I made it, he said it tasted like water. Just can't please everyone. All my presents backfired. First the curry for Tessan. Then I wanted to buy him a pastry, but it turned out to be bread with chocolate on top. I wanted to give the child a treat and left it beside him, but he didn't realize it was his.

MARCH 17

Listening to music in Masato's room, I went to another world, my other life. He is a kind of bridge, some thirty years old, long, scraggly hair arranged to cover the incipient baldness. He is gentle and silent, a voice that coos "zazen" with the tranquility of the wise. Yet he only talks about his stereo and his memories. Perhaps he thinks it's all we have in common. But his peace is real. He hitched across the States and Europe, can understand me, knows the road. The music is American. We drink coffee but sit on the floor. And it's very strange. The room is chilly, not cold, just so the skin tenses and tingles. Roshi is out, the music loud. I'm internalizing the music, really am the music, transported, transcending. I can't help smiling. I feel I'm bursting, vibrating up and down my spine.

Mio-san took photos. I looked at mine and was strongly hit by having seen it before. In Masato's room, looking at the albums, I felt I knew all these people well, but couldn't place them. Odd.

March 18

Jiko-san out chanting sutras. I have tenzo to myself, everything fine.

March 19

Again alone in tenzo. I give myself plenty of time to do everything and find the cleanup goes as quickly without Jiko as with him. In the afternoon I read and meditated. I come down to a very calm place. Thoughts aren't fluttering around unbidden and I just do what I'm doing. It's very peaceful not having to talk. Mio-san is the only one who is in. I find I like him very much. He used to seem so intimidating, as if he were looking over my shoulder. I know he accepts and respects me; maybe that's the difference.

Go Roshi brings us each back little cakes. I'm very touched. More than a big present, to have taken the time to think of us and want to give us a little treat, is so very kind. I spend a long, long time ironing his kimono. Could have waited til morning but thought he might need it this morning.

Today dawned totally different. I knew when I got up that I'd be grumpy. I felt I hadn't slept enough, though it was more than usual. Into tenzo and Jiko wouldn't shut up, spouting nonsense, and I forgot to take Go Roshi the kimono. The marmalade that I knew Mio-san was looking forward to didn't turn out right. I put out the wrong rice, but it was tasty. Jiko ruined it by boiling and boiling it. I washed my hands of it when he wouldn't stop boiling it, but he told everyone it was my fault for doing the wrong rice. I had been proud that when I did the rice it was always good. So I'm annoyed, and still more annoyed at being so petty in giving a damn about rice. Back to sleep for two hours and the world is brighter. Yesterday I was so together, calm, big mind; today so trivial and frazzled.

Keep at it, m'dear.

MARCH 20

For a day that started so awkwardly, yesterday mellowed out nicely. I like working in silence, watching my breathing. Mio-san and I ate lunch in the kitchen. It was much nicer than the cold, dwarfing dining-room. It's hard to talk to him (language), but his good nature shines through.

Yesterday was the first day of spring. Mio-san hung out the flag. Birds sang, and the air was warm and dancing. We opened the windows, and I sat with Nakamuro in the sunshine. He is one of the most unselfconscious, wonderful people I have ever met. He's twenty but looks fifteen and knows many different disciplines. Body straight and supple, he bends effortlessly. It's a pleasure to watch him bow. He's always laughing, always helping, but never in a martyrish way. Always the kind word, ready smile, and gusty *"ohayo gozaimas"* [*good morning*]. Goodness is no effort to him, just an expression of his nature. He gave me a book and a painted fan as one gives a conversation.

I wrote 'Who am I?' I amn't; I am. In some senses am

and amn't. What sense is what? Is there any sense? It's all so confusing. I wish someone could just tell me all the answers. But I don't, really.

Jiko-san came home late, tired, his voice hoarse from all the sutras. The last couple of days, I've been rather ignoring him, having enjoyed my days of silence. Last night I listened and chatted enthusiastically, and to see his face light up made me feel ashamed.

I feel timeless, a kind of happiness trembling.

The child came to say goodbye. He reached out his hand, giving me a western-style handshake, said in English, "Bye, bye."

MARCH 22

Another quiet, peaceful day. It's raining. Twilight in the kitchen. The gentle snugness of warm and dry while the outside drips. Doing the ironing in long, smooth strokes. All day my breath is very slow and very deep, and everything seems to be a meditation.

I sit in the kitchen with my Japanese book. Mio-san comes down from chanting sutras and is poking around. "You are a great woman," he says. "*hai*" [yes]. I am very surprised. People have said that before and I can laugh it off. I know they only say it for irrelevant reasons—foreign and female. But he said it not in a flattering way, more like one speaking aloud to himself, not concerned with my reaction. I was so taken aback that I blushed a very deep crimson and could only sincerely say, "Thank you."

Got a letter from Mom. I've been watching the post every day. I had put my involvement here in academic terms and sounded more together than I feel. I will get down to that aspect and must see about books. It made me feel very happy that she understands and is resigned to my being away for a while, though would like if it wasn't so long. Says she was touched by my thanks for her sacrifices. I should have thanked her years ago. Puts me at ease. I think it would be great to go back for Christmas, then come back here 'til after summer. Funny, though, I know if I'd shifted the emphasis of my letter to a more spiritual one, that she probably wouldn't have been so accepting. Yet that's so important.

MARCH 24

The researchers tested me again. They didn't say anything. Just as well.

Jiko and I read sutra at Tetsuburo-san's house. Jiko has such a sense of fun and festival. He decided to turn it into a carnival. We brought all the drums, bangers, and clangers we could find. Bremen musicians. Tetsubun-san loved it. Trying to read sutra, we kept breaking down laughing. Jiko bought sake, and we drank and toasted and watched TV comics. 'Twas a grand night. This morning I whipped into action. During the last week, I've gotten used to getting right at the cleaning and getting it done quickly. Jiko was surprised, and it's hard not to just ignore him and take over. He leans against the fridge: "I've forgotten how to do the tenzo jobs. You've gotten stronger; you don't need me." I must not be overbearing. The tenzo is for both of us. But still he only leaned. Everything was done but the putting away, and I hoped he'd just do it. I began the laundry and the rice and finally asked him to put away the dishes. It makes me feel like a sergeant. I don't like that role; it would be terrible to get used to it. Working with Jiko is good for me. I can learn much from him, and he brings out in me many tendencies that I don't like but then I can work on them.

Tessan-san suggested that I go to Kannonji as kitchen helper with him. I would love it. I couldn't possibly be happier if I tried. He said to tell Roshi, asked Jiko to tell him. He didn't seem enthusiastic, maybe afraid of how it would alter his situation. Fingers crossed, but either way is okay.

Chosan this morning for the first time in a week. Wonderful to watch Roshi again.

MARCH 25

Last night we catered for a party of twenty. It went off grand. Tessai-san came. I was very glad to see him. Strange. He only criticized. Not like him. Hope nothing is bothering him.

I had a great time with Jiko. I used to think he is the variable factor. He is the only one who annoys me, therefore it's his fault. But in some of my moods he annoys me, and in some he doesn't. So I'm the variable factor. Thus I'm at least as much to blame and a lot easier to try and deal with.

Go Roshi left for Kannonji. When he got to the end of

the road, he turned round and waved his hat like a young boy going on a holiday.

March 26

At nine in the morning Tetso-san says, "Do you want to go to Kamakura?" Okay. And we're off, and a wonderful day it was. The sun shone. We went to see the big Buddha. There we were—in Buddha. I was very happy and excited, the blossoms' sweetness blending with incense. I felt a great yearning, a child calling his mother into the emptiness, hearing only the silence of his own voice. Oh, how I was aching for *satori [enlightenment]*. If only I could be a child and hear the silence of my own voice. Walking, there was only sunshine and fun. We were the only obosans, but their evidence was everywhere in perfectly swept paths. Bowing, they let us into the temples—free. Two excited giggling schoolgirls tried their English on me and asked for an autograph. We came back late.

PART IV

Korea

I packed my bag for my trip to Korea and went to bed, but slept little and got up early for zazen. Jiko-san very thoughtfully made me gemmai. Tetso-san rose from his bed (after a hard night's drinking) and drove me to the highway. He asked several drivers until he got me a lift to a stopover. There I'd scarcely put out my thumb when a family stopped. The father spoke English graciously and took me about 200 kilometres down the road. Though I knew it would be more practical to look for a long ride from a truck driver (the family kept making stops), I liked them and decided just to go with my feelings. He was interesting, a leftist who told me about Japanese politics and education. He had tried the monastic life thirty years ago but got too hungry. I was surprised at the imperialistic wave of desire to convert him, but I resisted it. The little girl, who never looked me in the eyes, practiced her high school English. On the Tomei expressway, we discussed the relative attractions of the Beatles. She was glad to speak English. They fed me, then drove me to a stopover to find me a lift. They invited me to stay with them in Sendai.

The next lift was with three guys, little English but much laughter. We stopped at a café, and they said there'd be few rides to Shimonoseki so maybe I should take the boat from Kobe. But I want to hitch, so they take me to a stopover near Kobe. There are no cars for Kyushu, so I agree, it's the ferry. While one buys me juice the others secretly get my ferry ticket. They write a note in Japanese to show people for directions, then ask the steward and my neighbours to take care of me. Tears prick my eyes. Sunset is beautiful.

After I arrive at Kyushu, I cross to the mainland, hitching. The driver drops off his load, then makes a special trip with me to the ferry. The kind man at the ticket office does mine specially; then I watched the sea 'til time to go. I talked to a gorgeous Swede (does acupuncture) but felt silly as his girlfriend was there. A Frenchman takes lots of pictures of me with sunset, etc., but his movements are sharp and desperate, and there seemed to be a terrible rage in him. He kept following me around, and there was something about him I didn't trust. I didn't want him to attach himself to me, but wasn't one obliged to help a desperate man? I didn't know what to do, so I left to do zazen.

Everyone in my section was kind, talking to me, feeding me. I fell asleep early but was wakened by the New Yorker on my left talking to the Londoner on my right. Larry was talking about women and wondering aloud if Buddhist monks were celibate. I didn't really want to talk to them but somehow, late in the night, I did, and found they were grand. Poor Larry is lovely, but lonely. They're going to Seoul. I couldn't believe it when Jack said he'd lived in Morioka two years, knows Richard-san.

When I arrived Saturday morning, it's raining and the visa office won't open til Monday, so I tried to decide whether or not to go to Seoul. Then I schemed, thinking that if I went to Seoul I could probably stay with Larry and

Jack, but they didn't invite me. They talked about people I should meet but only recommended a cheap place to stay. I'm surprised and then glad, because I had been scheming. It's better that a scheme should fail and that I should succeed innocently in something else. Anyway, I was sure that good things would happen. They offered to pay my train fare, but I wouldn't let them. However, I carried a camera through customs for them. The customs inspectors, of course, only bowed and waved me on, delighted with the gaijin monk. The money changers, too, were charming. With robes and a shaved head is the only way to travel. In the waiting room all the foreigners are clustered. By this time we are all friends, exchanging addresses and hugs. The Swede lives in Kyoto. I liked his girlfriend but he was inattentive to her. I decided to catch the cheap military train. Jack and Larry insist on paying for the taxi.

After a ride through magnificent countryside, we arrive in Seoul. A thin man with the eyes of a child asked me if I'm a Buddhist monk. When I say "Yes," he asks where I'm going, then weaving in and out of the crowd he beckons me, leading me I know not where. I follow him to a bus stop. Then from his briefcase he draws a slender black book, gold lettering, obviously often tenderly held. He writes in it, thrusts it into my protesting hands, and bundles me on to the bus. The girl lets me off as he directed, but I'm lost.

Spying a gaijin face, I ask him, does he know of Hillside House? He does and smiles a faint, impish smile. "Are you going to speak there tonight?" "No," says I, quite surprised. "I sometimes do," he says. He works for the U.S. Army. Another one, think I, a bit patronizingly. He soon dispels that, humbling me. It seems that he takes in street kids. (Makes me think of my street kids in Cuzco.) He spends $1500 a month of his own money on them. He makes them work or go to school.

I go home with him. The house is bursting at the seams with slightly scruffy, smiling lads. He tells me their stories, of street fights and prostitutes, pimps and gangs. They look like such innocent children. He chides them in English. They love the excuse to mock wrestle with him. A girl sits in the corner, a bouquet of flowers on her lap. They published an article in the paper about him, and he got a wad of proposals. This girl insists they're made for each other and keeps popping around with flowers. He ignores her. He tells me about professional matchmakers and how society is strictly hierarchical (status and age). One uses different word endings depending upon one's relative position.

He gets one of the kids to take me on the bus to Hillside House, but first he phones to make sure there's room for "a priest he's sending over." The divil! He didn't mention that I was female and Buddhist. Mrs. Francis looked openly horrified when she opened the door to me. No room at the inn. I offered to pitch my bag in any old corner. Then she relented. Hillside House is just for Army people and Christians. Well, you can't win 'em all.

That night, Saturday, was Bible night. There were a

bunch of straight middle-Americans and fervent Korean converts. Debby sat opposite me, kept staring at my hair (or lack of it). "Well, I suppose it's easy to take care of, but how could you shave your hair off?" she kept stammering, shuddering, gaping, aghast at my bristles.

After dinner was religious discussion. The subjects were naive and kept returning to the threat of Communism. The Koreans, though very ardent, obviously knew very little about Christianity. Afterwards they gathered around me, especially the Koreans, fascinated, bombarding me with questions. Of most pressing concern to them was not why I was Buddhist instead of Christian, but why was I a Japanese Buddhist instead of a Korean one. They repeated, resentfully, that they had had 36 years of Japanese occupation.

On Palm Sunday morning they invited me to a full gospel service with the largest congregation in the world. I'd never been to one, so I was game. Didn't the people ever stare! But the service was frightening. Thousands of people swaying, sighing. It made me think of a Paisley or Hitler performance. The sermon was interesting, making the promise best suited to an oppressed people, the promise of future rewards. "The Lord wants men with dreams," that is, men with desire. Forget this real world and dream. Be good and get yourself a reward—always "self." But the scale was awesome, simultaneous video and translation. Clean-scrubbed Pastor Malone, with piercing eyes and a limp handshake, approached us afterwards with offers of coffee. Downstairs in the coffee bar, the pastor who had been most stirring was surrounded by buzzing followers. She had risen at the end to exhort the congregation into a frenzied praise of the Lord. Catching sight of me, she knifed through the crowd around her. "Buddha, Buddha, Buddhist devil," she shrieked. "Out, devil, out!" banging me on the head, the back, the chest. Laughing, I assured her I was no devil. She'd recover herself, then flail at me again, tugging at my *rakusu [item of a monk's robes]*, looking imploringly for someone to confirm her urge to rip it from my neck. The Francises and Pastor Malone shooshed me out, embarrassed. They then took me to lunch at the base, that little oasis of imperialism.

Coming back in the afternoon, Miss Kim of the previous night was waiting for me to take me to see some temples. We went way up a mountain. (The bus driver wouldn't let me pay.) The setting was magnificent, in a niche between two jagged peaks, nestled among wispy clouds, a waterfall coursing down the mountainside. The temple itself is painted in many bright colours contrasting with the simple grey robes of the monks.

I was very surprised to see so many women, mostly old. It seems that, if they are divorced or deserted, this is a refuge for them. Good idea.

They have a custom of bowing before the Buddha; the extent of devotion is indicated by the number of bows but marathons don't interest me. If I was a Buddhist devil in the morning, in the afternoon I couldn't have been more welcome than the Buddha himself. They laid before me a vegetarian feast of Korean delicacies and invited me to stay. I declined, but these *bodhisattvas [helpful, compassionate persons]* were wonderful, their hearts so warm I could almost physically feel heat. Bowing, smiling, radiating good natures, they drew me into their room, urging me to put on socks. (A marvellous system of underground heating makes socks unnecessary. The cold is really the only thing that gets to me in temple life. . .)

There were two older-looking gaijins meditating there. I was intrigued. The man wore a Mexican jacket, his long white hair swept back, the air of an artist. The woman immobile in a subtle camel coat, silver hair in a tight knot. I thought they were leaving and rose. His eyes, startling blue, caught mine and we smiled at one another. When they came out, they told me that she was a Swiss swami who had studied yoga in India for 20 years. She was amazed that I had been accepted into a male temple with no fuss. She'd read that it is difficult. They offered to drive us down to the town, then offered that I should stay with them. When we were leaving the temple, the moon hung full and luminous. Mists curled around the temple spires. Over a loudspeaker we heard chanting, the echoes reverberating. The cliffs seemed to call to the forests, chanting in reply.

Virjananda and Jimmy (she called him "the dreadful druid") took me to their immaculate apartment, tasteful but not lavish. There were Persian cats, a balcony, azaleas, and a lemon tree. She was a truly ecumenical spirit—a blossom lay beneath a picture of her guru with palms beside it from

Palm Sunday mass. They were overwhelmingly generous, wouldn't let me pay for anything, kept trying to give me taxi money, lunch money, bought me vitamins and a T-shirt and wanted to buy more. She was a real inspiration, meditates four hours a day. She gave me many warnings and exhortations. We felt uncannily close. (She's sure we've been involved in a past life.) People used to take Jimmy for Irish because he was so droll. He also likes to drink, and I felt a great urge to join him in a bottle, but under Viraja's purer influence, I refrained. The Indians are really into renunciation, unnecessary as a permanent way but good training.

When I went for my visa (I had forgotten my passport!) I ran into many people I knew from the boat. One man came up to me, smiling a timid, Japanese smile, said, "I saw you on the boat; hope you're well." An American agitator leaps from the doorway saying, "You must be one of the people I read about." (Some foreigners in a Korean temple.) Next thing, he's telling me all about strikes, wages, working conditions in Korea. Interesting.

The visa people were charming, didn't even charge me. I even met an Irish bloke there.

Miss Kim and I met for lunch. The visa people had pulled apart the folded paper that Go Roshi gave me at my initiation. Underneath a lineage from the Buddha, Go Roshi had written something that neither Miss Kim nor her Buddhist father could decipher. Then the owner of the restaurant introduced herself as a Buddhist of some high rank, and she translated the words into Korean. Miss Kim's friend explained it to me in French, and I tried an English interpretation. Who knows how close my version is? It seems that Go Roshi chose the following phrases from Buddhist texts just for me: "The person who follows Buddha's precepts and laws will attain great enlightenment." Well, that could hold for anyone, but still there was a feeling of being in touch with something ancient, secret, almost magical.

I then bought a few gifts to bring back, got good and lost, but saw a lot of Seoul.

Jimmy came home from work, and we had a warm evening, sitting, chatting, drinking Campari. Reclining in luxury on the black leather sofa, we talked about austerity—a delightful way to do it. They filled me with determination. Viraja, by hand, strung beads which were seeds from the Bodi tree where the Buddha was enlightened. She laid them on a vial of Ganges water and other holy things (whose significance I didn't know), packed me a lunch and other treats. She tried to give me $20, which I refused but later found in my sleeve. We embraced. "We'll meet again; we have before," she said. She was soothing while I cried. "You have it," she said. I couldn't believe her heart. As I was leaving, she stood behind the bars of her iron gates, hands joined, eyes lowered, chanting a mantra for me.

How can I ever repay the world the goodness that has so guilelessly been extended to me? Surely there is no bad person in the world and so many with loving hearts. My eyes were watering. I was sad, but somehow not sad, as if I wasn't leaving and had always been there, and as if all the kind spirits in my life have been one, weaving in and out, so they were never far apart. Viraga is a wonderful woman with a deep and daily spirituality, a part of her every act. Yet somewhere she seems to feel something lacking, as if there was something she hadn't burst or a peak from which she had lowered. I thought, what if I'd gone with Larry and Jack? I'd probably have enjoyed it, but what happened was so much more important.

Viraja and Jimmy advised me to catch the train; that seems best, as I don't want to miss the ferry. Again, like a spirit, a little old man appears and takes me where I need to go, then disappears. In Pusan I get on the wrong road and lose lots of time, but I finally get a lift. It was a truck driver, a simple man. We had to wait ages for his cargo, while he kept talking about how I can sleep in his bed tonight. This makes me wary, but he's okay, takes a beautiful mountain road. It reminds me that Japan isn't all concrete and wire. It's exciting to be back on the road again but I have no regrets about returning to Toshoji. At 6 o'clock, with still a way to go and drizzle starting, I knew he'd let me out soon. I didn't worry. I knew from experience that something would work out.

He drops me at a terrible hitching spot, by traffic lights and nearly in town on the wrong road, but two women actually do a U-turn to pick me up. At the station the older one, who is from *Eiheiji [Soto sect's main temple]*, buys me an express ticket and presses 1000 yen into my hand for something to eat. The train is about to go, but again I have tears in my eyes. How are people so kind? I feel almost humbled before such generosity. I don't know if I'm capable of it myself.

I arrive at Toshoji at a respectable hour, not too tired. There's someone in my room, a new dormitory student, but this one is a woman, Mayumi-san. They put her into the kitchen for training with the idea that she is to go to Kannonji as cook. I'm also to go there, at least for the summer. Mayumi-san is tall and timid, often quivering like a startled rabbit. She's hard-working, quick to laugh, and a joy to have in the kitchen. But Toshoji isn't what she had in mind. She wanted time for zazen but instead is thrust into the kitchen. At first I too resented all the time not spent on the mat, considered it time wasted, but it really is only a greater challenge. Her hopes are pinned on Kannonji. The first few days she couldn't eat in silence; it scared her. She'd giggle and leave half her food. Now it's okay. It seems funny—she knows she's getting married in the autumn but not to whom. Go Roshi tried to fix her up, but she'd have none of it. I think she'd like to marry an obosan. She's 27 years old, has never had a job, was groomed only for marriage, i.e., cooking, sewing, flower arranging, and the tea ceremony. Eeyuk! I wonder what's behind her interest in Zen. Good on her for trying.

Jiko-san was to go to Tokyo, so Tessai-san's wife arrived to take his place in the kitchen. She had been kitchen helper for three years, and anything different from her style was "*dame*" [*wrong*] right down to the way I'd sit. Still, I had to admire her energy and orientation. She was basically right and not bitchy but only strong-minded and rough in asserting herself. At the same time, Yugi-san seemed too intent on corrections. She'd say the rice was too hard, he that it was too soft, and both would nit-pick about trifles. At times I could let it run right off me, but at other times I was definitely niggled. It's easy to see how little control I have and how firmly entrenched my ego is. These things couldn't have affected me but for the idea of "I." It helped to try distancing myself and to look at the conditions which caused each to be so critical. This is a point which I definitely need to work on.

I had great energy when I came back from Korea. I needed drastically less sleep. However, my meditations were very flighty, and I'd want to get up from them. I got a terrible pain in my left eye, and Jiko-san went to great trouble to find me a chiropractor and to bring me to her. She is excellent, and my posture already feels different. She's a spiritual person, though looking coolly efficient in her medical gown. Seeing my sewing in a plastic bag, she gave me a homemade purse for it.

PART V

Spring
1980

Last night after washing up and a very distracted zazen, we called on Tetso-san. Suddenly he says, "Let's go to Ginza." So we're off, himself, myself, and Jiko-san, cruising through the flashing lights, priests of the night. On to Roppongi, where we go to a bar, the Berni Inn. I haven't been in a bar since I lived in San Francisco. I feel I'm encased by this red wallpaper, English crockery, dart board, and the sound of "old boys" English interspersed with the clickety-clack of Japanese. Too subdued for a pub, it had supermarket music and more sherry than beer. "*Namu myo ho renge kyo*" *[the chant of the Nichiren sect]*, said someone as we passed—a strange sight, I suppose. Two Japanese approached us, bought us Irish whiskeys. Jiko-san was getting definitely looser, laughing, boasting of how wonderful Ireland was. Very comical. He was in his element, with whiskey and an audience. I enjoyed myself thoroughly, laughed and laughed. Tetso-san was quiet, seemed somehow out of things. He was drinking juice (was driver), but it wasn't only that. Jiko-san was a riot. Often as I've cursed the old devil, I actually miss him now that he's in Kyoto. When I was responding to circumstances with my ego, feeling put out by criticism, or when Takeo-san would lose his temper over nothing, I'd think of Jiko-san. "*Ii yo, nandemo ii yo. [It's OK! Anything's OK!]*." Totally unflappable.

This morning Takeo-san blew up at Mayumi-san because she was slow at making tea. At chosan she cried and cried. I could empathize but could also realize how ridiculous it is to be put out by one of his explosions. He's worried about his new temple and says himself that he's neurotic. Watching his face, I thought how truly wolf-like he looks when he pushes his mouth out like a muzzle. When he raises and knots his brow, adjusting his glasses, his eyes become small and beady. They're close together, like the eyes of a wild animal, and he jumps up and runs like a wolf. I went out of my way to be decent to him so that I wouldn't feel resentment over what I knew was my stupid "self-notion." It worked incredibly well. When they are barking at me, they are victims of causes and conditions, but when I am gentle and kind, they respond accordingly. Then they, too, are *yasashii hito [gentle people]* and it's impossible to bear a grudge. It's true that if you love your enemy you have killed him for he ceases to exist.

I thought I noticed changes since beginning Zen. It seems as if I'm laughing all the time, but I can't really remember how I was before. I think I've always laughed, but I don't remember laughing this much. Looking in my tiny, grease-stained mirror, I can never see all my face at once, but I think lines on my forehead have smoothed out. My hunchback posture has become straight. I was very surprised, though, when the chiropractor said, "You have an abnormal spine—it's perfectly straight."

Eshin-san said last night, "Your face is completely different from when you first came to Toshoji."

Takeo-san agreed and I thought, "Well, of course, I'm bloody well bald."

Then he said, "Your face is shining; it is an enlightened face. Your friends will be surprised."

I'm still trying to work out the best way to deal with correction and criticism. At first I thought, Well, at Kannonji it will be okay because there'll be no one over me. That was one of the attractions. Or, if I have my own dojo, then I can do as I like, etc. Well, I realized I simply can't always be boss, so I'd better figure out how to deal with it.

Then we were folding covers for the monthly newsletter and I folded a huge stack in half, which was wrong, and I had nearly finished redoing them when they told me I was folding them too wide. I had to start the whole stack again. Eshin-san said, "Even Soshin-san makes mistakes, even excellent lady." Well, that seemed so funny compared to my own self-image (where I'm constantly making mistakes and being corrected by myself or others) that I started laughing and laughing. It really seemed hilarious. Then poof, all tension was released. Doing the stack all over again didn't bother me. And it didn't smart when Eshin-san said "Soshin-san is good with her head but not with her hands." All was well with the world. If I can divorce myself from my ego enough to laugh at my mistakes, then I think this will be the most effective response. Now I'm eager for criticism so I can try it out.

While I was waiting at a subway station in a seedy part of Tokyo, I was looking at the daytime dead neon light, the sleeping seaminess, waiting for night. It's an attractive world because it's earthy and grubby, alive, real yet totally false without the pretense of reality. Vibrant throbbing music and bodies. I thought about the alternatives that confronted me when I first came to Japan last November—the usual job as an English teacher didn't interest me. Either monastic renunciation or sensory wallowing drew me. A soul seeking surrender? It was either accident or providence that the former happened first. Either way was a search for liberation—freedom from inhibition, from other people's values, from their suffocating puritan ethic born from the delusion of a retributory hereafter. Or else the other option, spiritual liberation, but from what? This one was hazier. Those who suffer want liberation from suffering, but I seldom suffer. My life has been wonderful, blessed. Who could enslave me? I did as I wished when I wished. Now I feel gratitude that this Zen way took me, because I consciously, fervently, could not be said to have taken it. Now I feel there is no turning back.

I've been reading an excellent book that draws the distinction between positive and absolute *samadhi [intense effortless concentration]*. This makes many things clearer. I understand the Go Roshi of dokusans and sutras, the Go Roshi of chosan and daily life. I understand why soji is so important and have slipped naturally into positive samadhi in the kitchen.

Someone said that we must take care of things simply because they exist. This occurred to me as I was sweeping the floor. In the dust pile there were 16 grains of rice and two tiny crawling things that didn't need to die. It felt neither good nor bad.

I look at the clock. It is two o'clock. A long time later

I look at the clock and it is only two o'clock. It is always two o'clock. I feel a great peace.

Preparations are almost finished for Eshin-san's ceremony. Tomorrow he will be a priest. The ceremony is very simple and thrilling. Outside hondo the monks bow, then we file slowly in. Takeo-san beats the hell out of the drum in a heart-pounding chase intensity. I clack two pieces of wood. Eshin-san holds a fan. Ping bell, clack wood, bong deep resonant drum. Everyone bows. Eshin-san does various bows, receives the stick from Jiko-san and holds *mondo [the asking and answering of Zen questions]*. Each of us in turn shouts "Shak'shawan," and then each strides up, kneels before him, and addresses some Zen query. Then bowing, retreating, we roar "chincho." The loudness of my voice startled everyone, especially me. I enjoy bellowing out. My questions are: "What is emptiness?," "What is Buddha nature?" "What is man before he is born?" After having them answered, I'm afraid I'm still not much clearer in my mind. . . . Then more bowing. We each in turn offer our congratulations. Pronouncement from Go Roshi. We bow, and it's over.

Nakamuro-san sits with his fan, all athletic tension. Takeo-san once said that I was like a mirror, reflecting back impartially whatever was in front of me. But I didn't really know what he was getting at until, while watching Nakamuro-san, it became clear. He is beautiful. Sitting like that, he must be in deep samadhi. He's always happy and helpful, vibrant with energy while there so profoundly tranquil.

I was physically born in 1955. Can I die and be born this month of *Showa 55*? *[1979–80, the 55th year of the reigning Showa emperor, Hirohito]*

KANNONJI, IWATEKEN
MAY 2

The second day of the fifth month of 1980. Twenty-two days before I celebrate a quarter century.

Sesshin has begun.

Dokusan. I did mu with all my heart and all my soul and all my being. Everything was squeezed out until my head touched the floor.

"Is it your mind or your heart or your body saying mu?"

"I don't know." Tears are flowing without reason; I laugh without reason.

"What is the difference between I don't know and mu?"

"No difference." Go Roshi whacks me.

"Ouch!"

"Who feels pain?"

"I do."

Then, when I'm not looking, he jumps up, embraces me. "*Bikkuri shita!*" *[You surprised me!]*. I tumble backwards, laughing. He holds my hand tightly, my thumb.

"This is I don't know."

"I know."

"You must see mu in everything." I leave dokusan, crying and laughing, with Tachibana Sensei apologizing for his English translation. That's okay. He encourages me.

I go to dokusan with Kobai-san.

"Where does mu come from?"

"I don't know—how can it come from somewhere? It doesn't have a place."

Kobai-san is very fish-like, cold comfort.

"We've all struggled with the problem."

"It comes from me," I told her.

"If that's your answer, go to dokusan."

In we go again. Go Roshi says "*zenzen wakaranai*" [*"You don't understand at all."*].

I'm crushed, devastated. Roshi says, "Next time, come alone."

After lunch we rest. I'm crying, feel wretched, forlorn. I can't do it. Tessan-san has such strength in his mu; the fellow in white has such persistence. I couldn't keep on like him (I take big pauses between mu's). He thumps his head like little Sandra [the most disturbed child at Glencraig], bleating and beating. I lie down, weeping and mu-ing and half sleeping. I resolve not to go to bed that night or any night until *kensho* [*satori, or enlightenment*].

Going into zendo, I hear Go Roshi say something about Soshin (probably saying, "I was wrong; she's hopeless"). I'm called to dokusan. I feel so dejected, empty-minded. It doesn't even occur to me to wonder why Go Roshi wants me to come alone.

"*Mu—do? [How is your mu?]*"

I mu for him with all my strength, raising myself high and squeezing every bit of breath into mu until my head touches the floor.

"Once more again," he says in English. (He doesn't speak English, but I don't register surprise.)

I do so.

Then "Once more again."

My first and only thought was "He may make me do this for ages." Then he jumped at me, grabbed me—"This body is *muji [the figure of mu]*, this head, eyes, ears."

Suddenly I'm laughing and crying muji. I don't even realize "Now I am muji," but I simply was muji and everything around me.

And he hits different parts of my body. "This is muji." Count 20 in muji—20 parts of me, 20 muji in Kannonji, all around me. We're holding on to each other, laughing and laughing. "Heart muji," he says, thumping me. "And Go Roshi's heart muji," I say, belting him back. We're embracing.

"*Kensho shita [You have realized your Buddha-nature]*," says he.

I'm surprised. I was too self-conscious even to know that it was kensho. Only when I got outside and was looking at everything and really seeing mu did I finally know. Suddenly I understood why we must take care of things just because they exist; we are of no greater and of no lesser value.

At dinner the only words spoken aloud rang in my ears, "*Maura-san go kensho itashimashita [Maura has seen into her Buddha Nature]*."

At first I was so exhausted I felt neither joy nor sorrow, just relief. The next day I was ecstatic, couldn't stop smiling. Then all was as before—or at least, so it seems. Everyone tells me I look different. It's hard to be sure. I can't be bothered looking for big changes. I began the koans and flew through about twelve. Maybe they came easily because of my reading. I don't know.

After the kensho itself, a wonderful thing happened. That morning I had been fed from the strength of Tessan-san's and the others' mu's. Now that I had been "passed," as it were, I felt the desperation in their calling and I put all my strength into mu. With each breath in I thought, "Tessan-san is—" the huge breath out was "MU!" I called and I called to him. He went to dokusan and had kensho. There was still work to be done. Tessan-san and I cried and cried to the other monk. He answered, wailing. In harmony we shouted, trying to urge him harder and harder. I lost myself completely. I was him, Tessan-san, mu, all dissolved. But he didn't have kensho. I resolved that if he stayed up late, I wouldn't sleep but would urge him on. He didn't stay up. I was exhausted. Everything was expended. My throat was raw. I lost my voice, couldn't speak for two days. Still I tried calling to him the next day. The other head priest thought it strange and asked me to stop.

I wonder if Go Roshi judges by the right answer or how it's done. Probably both. I hope I'm not cheating myself by knowing some of the answers, but am afraid that I am. Koans were great fun. Go Roshi and I dissolving into laughter, he jumping up, careening around the room, hiking up his kimono to take a dive into a fictitious sea. It was so much innocent play. Yet I felt I wasn't going deep enough.

At the end of sesshin was Go Roshi's *teisho [Dharma talk]*. He spoke about me, said of the 20-odd foreigners that he'd helped I was the purest. He felt me to be like his child and wanted me by his side until he died. He said his plan was to make Kannonji an International Zen Centre for me. He turned to me beaming, "*Wakaru? [Do you understand?]*" (He never addresses the audience in teisho.)

"*Wakaranai. [I don't understand.]*" I had to reply. I love that man so dearly that I almost cried when Tessan-san told me what he said. Still, I can't see myself living always in Japan, being an obosan. Though it would be a good life for me, I'm just not that pure.

Go Roshi left and we began to settle into a routine. Tekkan-san and Kas'ko-san were still here. I fixed myself a room in the loft of a storage hut. I love it. Up high I feel myself to be a bird in my nest. All around the eaves birds wing and poke, calling. Two huge windows and sliding door give good light and ventilation. It smells so wonderfully of wood and now of tatami. Of course they all thought I was quite mad, but Tessan-san now says it's the best room. I climb in and out a window, commuting from the main temple.

One afternoon, on a whim, Tekkan-san took us up the mountains looking at blossoms. We picked many wild plants, brought them home for cooking. Gathering our dinner in the sunshine from nature's abundance somehow all seemed to be as it should be. Tekkan-san can be so gentle and always totally immediate and involved in what he's doing. This makes him brutally honest and when angered he is totally angered. It really annoyed me, though, to hear everyone putting him down, bitching behind his back. Not a soul stood by him—only Kas'ko-san, who could hardly be said to be a separate soul.

Tachibana Sensei took us (Tessan-san and me) on a grand outing. We went to another temple. It's much older and much more beautiful than Kannonji, but really made me appreciate Kannonji more. We're very free here, plenty of time for zazen. They do little zazen, only maintenance. We saw some very beautiful sites. I felt possessed, no longer human (or extremely human); an incredible energy was surging through me, sparking, flashing, a pure joy. He is an extraordinarily good and kind man.

Last night after dinner Tessan-san played the guitar. Me sitting on the floor, drab grey kimono, bare head, bare feet, doing my embroidery. He singing from the depths of a world of memories and dreams, his journey and love of life. Yet there was only that moment, rich and vivid. He made up a crazy song about Soshin-san cooking delicious pumpkin even if it was a little old and hard. We laughed like drunkards who can hardly remember why. He's so Japanese, yet a dropout (as he says)—two years travelling, playing his music, yet his ideal is the little woman on whose pretty face he can gaze as they both sit sipping tea. The dear little woman for whom he will fight all day so that he may relax, bathing in her innocence by night. Doesn't he need some education!

Women really are repressed here, forced into the mold of a giggling innocent. At first I rather enjoyed the surprise and admiration with which I was treated. Now I feel its oppressiveness, for it's only because I'm female. My heart went out to Kobaisan. She wished she could sit as freely and naturally as I, but couldn't. Such a simple thing. Always raised to sit like a lady, she was too self-conscious to be merely comfortable. It's odd, though, that she too said I look Japanese. I don't understand how so many people can say that. My eyes are distinctly round and coloured; if I had any more freckles I'd have a suntan.

The only change I can put my finger on since kensho is in reading *ookyo [the sutras]*. Now I love to shout in a big booming voice. Previously I simply could not. It's such a relief to really shout those sutras, lose oneself. (I could even sing at Tekkan-san's party.) I finally realize the value of ookyo, but it must be done loudly, then the breathing is very benefi-cial. The "screamers" in Ireland possibly did catch on to something effective, although they seem to lack the integrative benefits of a 2,500-year tradition. I can see shades of many therapies in zen. I've started chanting "*Kanzeon, namubutsu, yobutsu u in . . .*" *[the Kannon Sutra]* while I'm working. It regulates my breathing, and I can work with less distracting thoughts and a greater sense of oneness with the work.

I planted veggies, built a compost retainer, am preparing new beds. I feel such a peace puttering around in the dirt with all the wiggly, slimy, ugly little creatures. The creatures digging and fertilizing the garden and worth no more or less than I. I'm careful about them now; try not to disturb them, carry them to appropriate homes when they take over indoors. At first I was put out that Kobai-san was doing the kitchen, but it's worked out perfectly. I'm learning more about Japanese cookery and get to work in the garden. I'm very, very, very happy.

grateful

warmth

I stood in the rain for the longest time without getting wet. Nobody knew. It was my koan. The rain noises were on cement, on stone, on my plastic mac. The bird in the apple blossoms shook the moisture from its feathers and sang. I, in sympathy, shook in my mac and was silent.

To become is not to annihilate. To become the quarrel does not really stop it. It both stops and continues it. Wet and not wet. Is and is not.

How can one be Buddhist and not be socialist? How accept and allow the perpetration of a system based on desire? A system that functions as trigger and effect of the desire for money and commodities. A system that, to feed itself, must resort to crass commercialism and ever spiraling desire.

I wonder sometimes about Kobai-san's relationship to her own sexuality. She is staying with us until a husband can be found for her. She's apparently not worried about facing her future as the servant of a total stranger and has no idea at all of marrying for love. At first I thought perhaps she had come looking for a husband. She seemed to know nothing about Zen but talked incessantly about how hard it would be to marry someone without any hair. Tessan-san, she says, is her favorite but she told him that she didn't like men, that she was afraid of them. Often she would avert her eyes from me, or put a book in front of her face, laughing, saying my looks were too seductive. One night she said something to Tessan-san, using a word normally only used between lovers or close friends. He was furious, railed at her without letting up for fully an hour and a half. Banging the table with his fist, spilling the soup, stubbornly refusing to eat, threatened to call Go Roshi, and said she was welcome to leave. Kobai-san barely spoke. She sat meekly, eyes down, fiddling and folding a crease in her apron. She seemed neither particularly cowed nor perturbed. I, of course, couldn't understand and couldn't possibly imagine what could provoke such a reaction. Tessan-san's entire face was transfigured, almost unrecognizable, fascinating. His eyes burned into her. He seemed not to blink, every muscle in his body tensed, knuckles turning white as he gripped the table. It was all that seemed to support or restrain him. The following day she apologized and no tension seemed to linger on either side.

Yesterday Tachibana Sensei brought me to a jazz coffee shop. Good feeling to it. The waitress said, *"Mora-san desu ka?"* [Are you Maura-san?] I was shocked. How did she know my name? It turned out that she is a friend of the editor of the local newspaper, who apparently spoke highly of my English. The result is that she, her sister, and a friend will come every Sunday to Kannonji for English lessons.

It seems that many American jazz singers come and she wants to be able to talk to them. She was delightful and I think we may be similar souls—rare enough around here. She gave us free cheesecake and promised to take me to big concerts in Tokyo and anywhere I wanted in the area.

Funny. . . . I thought of ringing Richard-san; then I met him. I wrote a letter to Jiko-san and found his waiting for me. Then a couple of coincidences with Kobai-san. Now Kobai-san is convinced I can read people's minds. The telepathy between Jiko-san and me was often extraordinary, but I have certainly no special powers. Kobai-san asks me if I chant ookyo only for myself. Of course, for whom else? But she is trying to invest me with some kind of mysterious character.

MAY 24

My birthday: Working in the garden, sure that today would be like every other day, but not particularly bothered.

"*Gomen kudasai [What is called instead of knocking].*" I went to the door. A telegram. For me. I've never had one in my life before. In inscrutable *katakana [phonetic script used for foreign words]*, it said "Good Morning, Happy 25th birthday," addressed to Soshin O'Halloran Sama, from some woman in Tokyo—I have no idea who! How did she know my address, age, Buddhist name? Who could she be? Possibly the chiropractor. . . .

I made banana pudding. Tessan-san said, "What, no cake?" I pointed out the absence of an oven. The closest we could come was "hot cakey mix." He made a huge plate of plump, delicious, greasy donuts. He brought the stereo into the kitchen. There was great fun and love in the air as we prepared. Me in my long ceremonial gown dancing to Steely Dan on the tatami. We split one beer three ways. Tachibana Sensei remembered the date and brought me a radio. What a man! "Do you like jazz?" said Tessan-san. "Yes," said I, while thinking to myself, I'd like Phoebe Snow. Phoebe Snow it uncannily was. Often, with very simple things like that, I think of something I want and it just comes. Strange.

Sitting around the table we whipped a candle from an altar, balanced it in an ashtray. Tessan-san played the guitar. I sat crosslegged in my robes, smoking a cigar and laughing at it all. A grand birthday.

MAY 25

The next morning, Monday, Tessan-san and I had our

first disagreement. On Sunday we had gone to the hot springs with Tachibana Sensei. I had, as usual, bought a little something for his kids. Tessan-san muttered, "Oh, I must get him something, too." Next morning he launched into a lecture on why it was bad for priests to give presents. They were only supposed to say "thank you" and take. I was furious. The cheapskate, trying to twist things around. He said priests don't have money except what is presented to them to spend on their needs. I have very few needs, and I would damn well give presents until I really did have no money, instead of not doing so because I shouldn't have money. I shouted and argued, tripping over myself with rage. Then he rambled on and on without connection about various things, never outright attacking me, but saying, "You will get sterner with yourself," implying but not saying that I wasn't stern enough. He divided and separated us by saying, "You still have your foreign ways" and "I hate to have these discussions with a woman." I was so angry I knew that if I spoke I would cry and corroborate the "woman" bit. So I glared, bored into him with every iota of anger I could muster. I shredded him with my eyes. Merciless.

Finally I had to start cleaning but couldn't stop mulling the whole thing over. Why had I become so terribly angry? It was really a small thing. I've seen him now, arguing with everyone, and Tetsuro-san had warned me about his "new-priest-that-knows-it-all" ways, so it was easy to foist the blame on to him. But my reaction was exaggerated. I needed release. He was on his way out to school. It was the wrong time, but I called him anyway. "I was very angry with you. I'm sorry. Sometimes you act as if you know everything and nobody else knows anything." I don't know if he caught the latter. "Your face was terrible," he said, "your eyes—" We laughed. It was okay. We're human. Since then I've purposely discussed Tachibana Sensei's present. Thankfully, no reaction.

I have so little control really. The day before, I was bursting with joy. Every twitch of the breeze, ripple on the mountain, whine of machinery, everything delighted me. Then, boom, I explode at poor Tessan-san.

MAY 26

Kobai-san has been having a heavy dose of *makyo [distorted perceptions from zazen]*. She hears footsteps, sees many priests, sees herself as a young girl in a red skirt among the flowers. Hears ookyo and our voices. Seems to have a fixation around ookyo. She can't do it loudly in the morning but since the onset of makyo does it loudly each evening. The obosans may have to do with her fear of them, as in Toshoji she feels there are people behind her.

Once she realized it was in her mind, she felt better. I slept beside her for a couple of nights. Zazen really does change consciousness. Just as consciousness-changing drugs may prod hallucinations, so will zazen. I'd love to understand the whole thing.

MAY 28

Kobai-san seems better now. Though I can't talk to her, I'm very fond of her. She is so honest and candid—inhibited but not too inhibited to admit it. She wants to touch us, but can't. I try to make light of it, chase her around the room, threatening to tickle her. She doesn't know what to do. She says I have many faces: beautiful, pretty, angry, child-like, frightening. People react to me differently of late. It's strange sometimes, my face is too bright, like glaring sunshine. The child said I look totally different and now look Japanese. The foreigners came and were fascinated, stared too long—perhaps it's the shaved hair. No, it's really odd. I look in the mirror and don't know. I don't know how I looked then and how I look now. It'll be interesting when I go home for Margy's wedding—hope that little sister of mine is doing the right thing.

MAY 30

I had my first zazen "student," Richard-san's English student. He came to meet me. Tessan-san invited him to my Sunday morning classes. It was a fiasco. His English is too good. I said I had no time. He asked if I had time to talk about zazen each day. That was my duty. I said there wasn't much to say; it was a question of doing, but I'd give him time before soji. He wanted to know all about English manners and customs. He came the next day. I talked Zen at him. He didn't seem interested. I felt tricked. He only wants free daily English conversation lessons. I'd give him a few more days and then get tough. Next day he asked me to teach him how to sit. I did. He was so enthusiastic, so hopeful, it gave me real pleasure. Then he stopped coming. I truly mustn't be a bodhisattva, for I felt a little relieved. Then he came again. I'm glad.

JUNE 1

For Tachibana Sensei's birthday I pushed my exhausted self, spent quite a bit on food and presents, cooked and cooked, decorated the sitting room. He phoned.

"Happy birthday," I said.

"But it's not my birthday."

"Ha, ha, you can't fool me; I remember you said May 31st, a week after mine."

"A mistake. I meant March."

What a laugh! So he went along with it and we had a smashing party. Then off to the jazz café. The atmosphere was of the wee hours of the morning, snug, not quite asleep, a warm cradling sensation.

The wasp and lady-bug invasion taught me plenty. *Busshari-to ["The Hall of Buddha Relics," where ashes of the cremated are enshrined]* was overrun with them. Tessan-san sprayed. I brought up the Hoover, but it seemed wrong to vacuum up the live ones and have them suffocate in its dusty bowels. What to do? One by one I picked them up on the shovel and put them outside. It took ages. Each time I cleaned Busshari-to, it was the same. It was annoying but I had to. Yet somehow, in an ever so slight shift of focus, it brought home to me that I am no more and no less than, and not separate from, a fading ladybug or a dying wasp. Respect life, not because it's right or good or moral, but because it is. It's a nuisance to pick up the sesame seeds one by one when everyone has finished eating goma *sembei* [*sesame crackers*], to eat the potato peels that the others don't like, to chase and rescue even a single grain of rice. That the single grain of rice is all rice is all things, is nothing, is valueless, that there is no value and not-value great or small; only is. As I swept up the corpses in Busshari-to, I realized I was distinguishing life from death.

Each day in the garden I explain to the weeds that they do not really die; they change form, as they are doing anyway. Yet I distinguished. I didn't want to pick up the cadavers with my fingers. Clean-dirty, dead-alive, even plant-animal (for handling dead flowers caused me no qualms). So for training I made myself pick up all the dead flies, spiders, moths, and bugs that crossed my sweeping path. Not really so bad after all, though I'm still more inclined to use the broom. Have several times just forgotten and picked the thing up.

I love getting filthy in the garden. The others get disgusted. I had an interesting dream. Rushing to work in a place like Dunster [restaurant in Cambridge, Mass., where she worked in 1979], I jump off a bridge-like thing and land on a table where a nun is selling potato cakes. My filthy shoes first, then I sit on them. I begin to eat the ones I've destroyed; she gets almost hysterical: "You can't eat them; you stood on them, yuck, dirty." I'm in a hurry to work, trying to eat and explain that I dirtied them so I must eat them; no one else will, so they mustn't be wasted. She's in a flap. Finally she calls Reverend Mother, who is also upset, but acquiesces. I, thinking, how stupid, wolf the cakes, dash to work. I explain to the cook why I'm late. He laughs. Obvious dream elements—Buddhist/Catholic contradiction; the potato skins I made myself eat; Tessan-san saying my feet were dirty, the endless waste that revolted me at Dunster.

Sesshin Toki [time for intensive zazen]. Someone made a mistake on the announcements and hardly anyone came. Go Roshi was not perturbed but changed sesshin into zenkai, so fewer sittings of zazen. Pity.

It was a pleasure to see him again, an inspiration to watch him peeling an orange; he was deeply involved in the tearing of each vein. How many oranges had he peeled in his life, yet still enthralled! Watching TV. When I first came to Tokyo, I heard the TV from his room. I thought, "How insensitive his wife is," felt somehow superior to this soap-opera–addicted woman. She moved out, and still the TV blared incessantly. Roshi himself watched it. "Oh, well," thought I, not really knowing what to think. Now I could watch him watch. He is so totally engrossed, a child pulled right into the screen. Beautiful. I remember how the Ryans used to invite Scott to watch TV so they could watch him. Go Roshi was the same.

During the zenkai I was given a koan about a man digging a hole and not getting to the other side. Tetsuro-san's translation left out the fact that the question was "Why couldn't he get through after having dug the hole?"

Go Roshi said my answer was that of an unenlightened person. I was crushed. It tore open all my insecurities about whether I really had kensho or not. Later I gave a similar answer—that when digging there was only now, no after digging, therefore no through, only in the tunnel and digging. Roshi said that was the answer to a different kind of koan and explained that the man was universal and greater than any of his creations, therefore greater than the hole. Still, all my self-doubts were triggered.

He said the koans would get more difficult (a warning, perhaps), and he hopes I run away to Ireland (laughing). He asked me to stay ten years.

"I don't know," sez I.

"Nine," he bargained.

"Eight and a half," I offered.

He offered me his room at Kannonji instead of my loft.

"*Yuck, iranai*," [*I don't need it*] I said, and he laughed. Always laughing. What could possibly disturb him?

During teisho, he said that I alone could become the greatest woman priest. (However, the competition is not exactly overwhelming.)

The final day of sesshin/zenkai, the TV people came to film me. They were fascinated and alarmed at my room. "Aren't you afraid of ghosts?" is the universal reaction. Even educated Japanese seem to be obsessed by ghosts. They eeked and ooed and generally fussed outrageously as they lugged the camera and lights up the ladder to my loft. They were funny. I liked them but felt silly talking about myself.

"Why did you do Zen?"

I told her the story about Ciaran [an old friend who became a Buddhist monk in England]. Afterwards, thinking about the question, it seemed like something I never decided to do but something deep inside that I knew I was going to do, not with a sense of determination but in the same way that I know Monday comes after Sunday. Inevitable.

Kobai-san was funny after seeing the documentary thing. She started calling me *Kannon-sama [Blessed Kannon, the Buddhist Saint of Compassion]*; she loves idols.

Go Roshi's 70th birthday-cum-book-publishing-event was at a hot springs hotel. I barely finished my present for Go Roshi in the lobby below. Many masters had gathered for the occasion. They were beautiful men, radiant. Each gave a speech. At my turn I fumbled and blushed; how could I put into words what I felt? Lear's youngest daughter. Tessai-san's wife told me to give my present. I didn't want to in front of everybody, but I did while she blithered on about it taking three and a half months and me finishing while everyone slept. I was crimson. He passed it around.

The roshis were amazing, on the stage fooling around,

as innocent as babes. Those knowing sages, knowing it all, were leaving all knowing behind and just doing. There sure as hell is something in that Zen. Go Roshi, cancer-ridden, celebrating his 70th birthday. The night before, he chose his gravestone; tonight they hurl his tiny frame in the air, catching him three times. He laughs good-naturedly. I went to pour him a drink. He grabbed my hand, pumping it vigorously (they love an excuse to shake hands), saying, "Thank you, thank you," in English. I was crying.

I had to take my turn on the stage. Amazing—it didn't faze me to have to sing a song. I didn't use the mike but boomed around the hall with all the strength the ookyo had freed. I bobbed around making a fool of myself with the Japanese dancers. Okay.

Dear Mum, Margy, Scott, and Beth,

Phew! Am I exhausted! We had a sesshin where a bunch of people came to the temple. It culminated in a memorial celebration of

Roshi's 70th birthday, so there was a ton of work before and after the whole thing. The actual celebration was at a hot springs. So very Japanese, with the women all taking baths together and the men likewise. Then there was a big spread upstairs. Although I hadn't realized it, Roshi is very famous, and great Zen masters from all over Japan came for the occasion. (As usual, I was the only foreigner and the only woman monk. Only recently I learned how unusual my experience is when I heard of a German woman who bullied her way into a man's temple but was never allowed to wear robes or to be a monk. Interesting. Most temples won't allow men and women to study together.) Anyway, they're marvelous men, these old monks. They're like children, joking and playing. One old fellow gets up on the stage, a revered and respected Zen master, hikes up his robes, straps a pillow on his back and dances a strange dance about a "babe" on his back. Roshi just had a huge definitive book published, so that was also being celebrated and we were each given a copy. (Much of it is written in the script I've learned, so I'm struggling to read it.) They all took turns singing and of course I had to do an Irish solo. (Blush, blush.) Luckily they didn't know how the tune was supposed to sound.

The ladies were all swaddled in pastel kimonos. Several of them did one of their abstract (to me) Japanese dances. Then I was dragged up to join them. I tried to imitate them but they resembled *fluttering butterflies, while I looked like someone shovelling snow. The difference was much more than a pastel kimono.*

There was no doubt that it was a Zen party when, at the end, we went around from guest to guest graciously putting their leftovers into our boxes. We're already sick to death of them after only one day.

It's nice to be back at Kannonji again and to be living in the country. Although we're near the highway at the front, out back rice paddies spread to the mountains, punctuated by bamboo groves. Less romantically, the buildings are full of creepy, crawly creatures.

In the midst of the preparations for Roshi's ceremony, we had an entire day of interviewing and filming for television. They came again this morning to film my room at the top of one of the wood sheds. It's really just a platform, and the women from the TV studio were terrified they'd fall over, so they clung to the wall. They kept mumbling that they were sure living in such a room was good for my ascetic practice. In August I've been asked to give three talks about Ireland and about my life, during a three day UNESCO conference. . . .

Love, M.

JULY

My eye kept causing me trouble. Takehiko-san put in needles and electrified me, but the eye is as bad as ever. I went to an Occidental doctor, who gave me some drugs to mask the pain. I won't take them. I bought a massager. Maybe by loosening the shoulders I can help the eye.

KANNONJI, IWATEKEN
JULY 20, 1980

Dear Family,

. . . glad to get the invitation to Margy's wedding. It looks so official. Things must be hectic there. It's been that way here, too. We had dai-sesshin, the biggest sesshin of the year. However, the usual kitchen helper was called to Toshoji beforehand, and the other monk was busy learning to drive, so alone I did all the cooking, cleaning, weeding, flower arrangements, and sesshin preparation throughout this big temple. After all that build-up, I was exhausted, then did five days and four nights of zazen. But strangely, after the second

day of sesshin when I was most tired, I broke through a block and got a sudden, huge, unexplainable surge of energy, which took me right through sesshin, not tired at all. Now I'll take it easy for a couple of days before going off to the coast for this UNESCO conference. And soon after that I'll be heading off to Maine for the wedding. I leave Tokyo August 17th, so see you soon.

Last night, for a complete change of pace, some friends took me to a country festival. One of the mothers dressed me up in a kimono, binding my waist so tight I was sure my ribs were crushed. It was great fun, with all the little girls decked out in kimonos, beautiful origami chains festooning the streets. But it was so different from South American festivals, where everyone would get roaring drunk while they banged out the same tune on whatever would serve as an instrument, stumbling and stomping insanely til dawn. The Japanese version was much more restrained, prettier, understated, much bowing and fanning. Lovely, but I think there's a bit of the Latin in me.

After the festival the same friends took me to a jazz club in Morioka. The group had finished playing and were sitting quietly getting drunk by candle-light under the dark wooden beams of what could have been a Breton grenier. One of them was American and hadn't had a chance to speak English with a native in a month. When the gaijin in the yellow kimono with the punk haircut came in, he felt he had to invite us to join him. So we wined and chatted *into the wee hours. We must have squeezed in an hour and a half of sleep before getting up for zazen and sutra. I'm writing this after breakfast as we await the arrival of thirty school kids coming to learn zazen. Should be funny. Anyway, must iron my kimono, change the flowers and whip up to the shops on the old temple bike. See you soon. . . .*

Love, M.

JULY

My kid sisters, Kate and Margy, are both getting married! I can't believe it. I feel much too young to get married. Lately, I've been thinking of staying ten years to become a master. Then I wonder if I'll miss out on some love-type relationship. I'd be 34. But, really, I don't think it will be a problem. I feel that there'll always be men.

I worked hard on my koan and had a few really good sittings. I was wooden Buddha and flame. All must change, but nothing really changes, as it is always changing. As nothing really exists, how can it cease to exist? The flame is no more permanent and powerful than the Buddha. They are all muji. There is always change, change we perceive and that which we don't. We perceive change in relation to fixed ideas, but it's really not fixed, thus not a change. Words tricky, but inside it's crystal clear. A little breeze became a raging gale; it's changed yet not really; both are only particles of air in motion.

I did four nights of all night zazen, starting June 22nd, the longest day of the year and my longest night. It was incredible. The first night I kept thinking all beings are Buddha, could feel it. I felt totally purged, riding some high crest. The 2nd night I kept thinking no separation. The next day, pulling weeds, they were part of me but different, like the back and front of my hand are different but not separate. Taking a break, I drank a cup of coffee. It was like no other cup of coffee. It was me, like sucking my own blood, but more intense, as its familiarity was shocking. The third night "There is only here and now" reverberated in the corridors of my mind. The fourth night was bad; I kept nodding off. I love doing all night zazen. (I lie down for about an hour.) My eye went gamey on me. I want to do very hard cultivation. Already after only two days I've lost intensity and am as spiritually gross as ever (though I had a nice little samadhi this morning). I keep thinking that ordinary effort gives ordinary results. Before, I was looking forward to going home, but now it seems like an interruption.

I've been having some cases of telepathy. I got a beautiful letter from Jiko-san, full of Buddha and very supportive of me. He's going soon to his temple—Buddha and he are waiting for me—he underlined. The temple was meant for us, etc. He really is very pure, very good, but I wouldn't be into it at all.

Go Roshi came up for sesshin. I had been slaving. Tessan-san had most conspicuously not been. There were too many weeds. We were scolded. I couldn't stretch myself any thinner and resented Tessan-san, resented when I had to do all the work. All Kobai-san's and the little he had, was left undone until I did it. While he smoked, listened to music, I ceaselessly scrubbed, cooked, pickled, and did zazen, then hated myself for resenting him. If I was truly involved in my work, I wouldn't be looking to see what he was or wasn't doing, wouldn't be measuring and comparing.

Go Roshi asked if I could hammer. I said I could. Together we went out to nail up the donor plates. I did the top row, he handing me each one in turn. I was rather proud of how I handled a hammer. When we came to the bottom row, he did one. He licked the nail, and with two blows of the hammer it was firmly affixed. So we continued, I doing the top row—tap, tap, tap—he the bottom, strictly, smoothly. We laughed and giggled at my clumsiness. Each board seems funnier, our heads coming together like conspirators in laughter. Tessan-san came back from driving-school. He took the hammer from me.

"Man's work," perhaps he thought. He did it better

than I, so I relented but the fun dissolved. Roshi returned to his room.

I decided to do a really good sesshin and stayed up each night doing zazen. During the days Tachibana Sensei had to go to school, so no one could translate my koans. Sometimes I went to dokusan alone. One time Roshi asked me about my sisters' weddings and then when was I getting married and to whom.

The second night of sesshin, the young priest seemed near to kensho. He went to Busshari-to. I was doing zazen above him and came down to take a break. He and Nakanagi-san had joined one another in Jizo-sama's room [the room of the bodhisattva who looks after deceased children and prisoners]. As I gulped my coffee I felt a sense of mission. I'd help them that night. Going back in, their mu's were flagging. I started crying with them. All night we roared. When Nakanagi-san began to doze, I shook him, crying into his ear, holding him, guiding him to the window, anything that he might continue. The young priest kept going of his own accord. I had to stay strong, when we were all fading, had to bellow a mu that would resurge us. Mu seemed to throb in my *hara* [belly], seemed to be a pump surging up and down. I became them, them me, all only mu. It was deeper than anything that happened to me before kensho, first time I'd done mu 'til morning.

Nakanagi-san had kensho next day, but the young priest finished sesshin without it.

PART VI

Resuming

After a long absence, I resume. Ireland over, weddings, ups and downs. Margie's not so good but Kate's was a laugh—parties, singsongs with Chris, the best man. Me playing the spoons, all of us battering, rejoicing into the night. Cooking for weeks ahead. Orange ambrosia and mushroom soup forced on all who entered. I'm extremely happy about Geoff. I couldn't stop smiling throughout the ceremony. Many flirtations and reunions. Comforting to know that men are still falling in love with me and friends are still close. But it was hard to walk home alone by the canals after the last pint, the last bus, past the strolling couples, their greasy late night chips steaming from yesterday's newspaper. I had a lost feeling, wistful, not knowing for whom or what, for my practice that's not as good as it should be, for the lover, so wonderful, that I've yet to meet? Or was it just the whiskey and the damp? Who knows?

And who cares, for as time went on I felt less frantic, less constrained to live all that I was going to live in those six weeks. There was much love, deep warm womb love, coming from those I was afraid had forgotten me. It took a little time to bridge the gap, the missing years and sharing, but it was all there still. Much to do. They wanted me to give a talk on Zen; some wanted to train; the politics pulled me. So many places to extend myself, but first I must train myself, and rigorously.

Back at Kannonji, I was surprised to find that Eshin-san had run away. The stories . . . In a way I was relieved. My training would improve and their terrible pressure to marry me off in May would be gone. Apparently in my absence this plan was even more formalized. Tessan-san is kind but severe, teaching me ookyo, screaming at me. I can't understand the Japanese, don't know what I'm doing wrong. Tears come but they are like sweat, an excretion. Inside I'm not really affected. I don't dislike him (though he shouldn't take pleasure in his role), am not angry or really upset. This is the first very definite progress I can see. I'm grateful.

Dear Mum, Scott, and Beth,

Phew! Back in Japan at last! You must be back in Maine by now, Mum. Hope your trip was less eventful than mine. I got to London with no trouble except for the ton weight of baggage. Then going out to Gatwick I made every mistake in the book and ended up on a train that sailed gaily through Gatwick, hurtling out into the countryside as my plane prepared for take-off. Arriving at the desk in the airport, I asked the attendant what was the next one I could catch. "Sorry," says she. "This is an Apex fare, good for one flight only. Your ticket is now worthless." I nearly died. She must have seen my face falling nearly into my runners because she took mercy and said she'd pretend I'd rung up beforehand to cancel. That way she would only charge me the cancellation fee. But that was still £37.75, and sterling at that. I guess my face didn't rise much because she finally took pity. "Don't tell anyone or I'll lose my job, but I'll reissue your ticket." What a relief!

Had a stopover in Saudi Arabia. I only saw the airport, but it was odd to see the men in the lounge in full desert gear and the women hidden in their long, black tents. Our next stop was Hong Kong. I had a whole day there, time enough to wander around and be glad to be getting away from it. It's a huge, hot, teeming city, totally Asian in feeling despite the Western-style skyscrapers. I thought I was beyond feeling squeamish at marketplace sights after a year in South America, but I have never seen so many slimy things writhing, wriggling, being slashed, scraped and gutted, in any such a tiny area. Everyone seemed to be involved in some kind of carnage, but the day of sunshine did me good.

When I arrived at Tokyo, it was the middle of the night. I knew the gates would be locked at Toshoji, so I decided to snooze in the station until it was time for the early morning train north to

Morioka. I found myself a bench and settled in. I suppose every self-respecting Japanese has a home to go to, so my fellow bench-mates seemed to be mostly down-and-outs and drunks. Just as I started to doze, one rather inebriated character decided he had to welcome me to Japan and to practice his English.

I can guess what his contact with the tourist industry must have been since all he knew was "Hello" "No, thanks" and "Get lost." Then one of the better dressed ones, who was a mute, set himself up as my protector; he wouldn't let any of the other curious or friendly bums within yards of me. The shock came at one a.m., when the train station closed down. All the subways had stopped, and all at Toshoji were asleep. Using signs, gesticulations, and little drawings, my mute got it through to me that there was an all-night cafe nearby. There, for the price of one expensive cup of coffee, you could try sleeping to the thump of Japanese rock music. That seemed to be what all the clientele had in mind as they sprawled across tables or hunched in their chairs. At four a.m., when the station re-opened, my escort accompanied me back, ascertained my train, and sat patiently for another two and a half hours until he saw me on to the train. I was so touched by his kindness—and we couldn't even talk to one another.

When I got back to Kannonji, I was amazed to find that the monk who'd been here when I left in August had run away. (They always seem to run away rather than give notice.) Another fellow has been sent, at least temporarily. In Tokyo this one always seemed

136

surly and very bossy, so I wasn't exactly thrilled. But I just do what he tells me. He works like a wild thing, which is great. Luckily my Japanese is still terrible, because there was talk of giving me a crash course in ceremonies and leaving me to run the whole thing! So we'll see what happens with this fellow. He doesn't know any English at all, but so far we're getting on fine. But facing into this eternal winter, it crosses my mind that I must be crazy or masochistic or something. Oh, well—it sure as hell is good training. The Army couldn't be much tougher. Anyway, m'dears, I must go gather wood for the bath fire. Think of me when you turn on the central heating. (I'll try not to think of you at such a time . . .)

Love, M.

DECEMBER

December 3rd was the first anniversary of my arrival in Japan.

Shimo-san has been sick. Exaggerating. Looked like a pig peering from under the lurid pink blanket.

I went to dokusan. There was much questioning about letters and return dates. It seems that Go Roshi had a premonition I'd return before Kate's wedding. So much for premonitions.

I passed the koan of the big and little mountains. Now am free from desires, ambitions and attachments, can do real action, not just reactions, being led by the nose. No longer does he accept blindly but is free to accept or act because he can accept. It's real because it's the action of the real man.

The snow has started. It's still novel enough to be beautiful. It lies a white cushion across the mountain and rice fields. Somehow the world seems new, an infant, untainted, quiet, sounds absorbed by the snow. The mountains echo a deep silence pierced only by the occasional cry of a crow.

December 9

Hondo—dust, shoji and sweep; *Ue [upper levels]*—feather-dust & sweep; *A-Genkan [entrance where footgear are left]*—sweep; H-wind *Roca [hallway]*; Zendo —dust, shoji and sweep; kitchen, roca and dai-genkan—sweep, *renshu [practice]*.

December 10

Busshari-To 2, 3 and 4: Vacuum and do stairs, damp towel but not take down, dust walls.

Shimo-san has gone to Tokyo for 10 days. Whether he is here or not is equally okay. I'm amazed. In Toshoji he was the one spoiling influence for me. I didn't want to be stuck here for the winter, didn't want to be with him, didn't want to do takuhatsu. I wasted much valuable time and energy pondering how to avoid doing these things. Now I've asked to do takuhatsu—even alone. (I'm sure there'll be times I'll regret that.) Life with Shimo-san and winter are fine. He was sick for a few days and rather repulsive. The combination of his expression and Asiatic features gave him a distinctly Down's Syndrome appearance. After he recovered from his sniffle he was marvelous, always laughing, writing me little songs, helping me at every turn. I have to admire his hard-working nature and generous heart.

Tachibana Sensei had me over at his house on Sunday. We sat under the kotatsu watching an old black-and-white English movie. It was bliss. Cream cakes, apples, and brandy. There was no more in the world to ask for.

These last two days, alone, I slept later than usual. The first day I forgave myself. "It's merely conditions; you'll get down to it." Today I was disgusted with myself. My zazen is not good or strong enough for nonsense like missing a sitting. In fact my zazen seems very bad. I know that is only a thing of my own creation—"good zazen/bad zazen"—but it reflects where I'm at, which is a pretty unadvanced state. Nuts. Get down to it!

Dear Mum, Scott, and Beth

. . . Back here the picture is still unclear, but will undoubtedly sort itself out. The new monk here has a bit of a chip on his shoulder, as he's been a zen student for five years but hasn't managed to have kensho yet (the initial breakthrough). So he feels that all the younger trainees who've had kensho have to be shown that they're not as great as they think they are. At Toshoji all he did was argue, so I decided to make things easier for myself up here by doing things his way from the start. The first few days he pampered a cold, sat all day beneath a pink blanket, looking for attention. I'm afraid I was less than sympathetic and Florence Nightingalish. However, he recuperated and attacked the wood-chopping with admirable vigour. Soon my attitude towards him completely changed. I did as I was told, so there were no arguments. We actually had great fun in broken Japanese. Then this monk had to go back to Tokyo on business, and I was left here on my own. I was managing morning and evensong in dubious Japanese. (The lengthening or shortening of a syllable can change the whole meaning, so who knows what I was saying?)

Last night, just as I was finishing dinner, a shout came at the door. A monk had arrived from Tokyo to keep me company for the next ten days. He's a bit of a character. I remember that last summer he asked to become a priest and Go Roshi threw him out on his ear.

I wonder what happened in the meantime. He talks to himself and grunts a lot and does everything the opposite way from the other monk and insists he is right. I wish there were some definitive authority on the subject. It's confusing changing everything around with every new face. Next month will be the begging, so there'll be a bit of a gang here. Maybe by then they'll have found someone else.

The weather has turned quite cold, but I wear my Goodwill duds under my kimono and scarcely feel it. I look a big lump, but who cares? Tachibana Sensei [the local high school English teacher] *takes good care of me. Last Sunday I went to his home. We watched an old Gary Cooper movie, ate cream cakes, and drank brandy. I was in my element, loved being with a family on a Sunday afternoon. Of course nowhere nearly as good as my family, but still very warm and kind. . . . Happy, happy, happy Christmas!*

Love, M.

DECEMBER 11

I finished dinner and was reflecting on the fact that it was one year to the day since I became an obosan. Led to the inevitable pointless analysis of change, progress, etc., getting nowhere fast. Then a shout came at the door. Go Roshi had sent help! This bloke is a right character. He does everything differently from the way Shimo-san does them and insists he's right. He was here last summer, asking to be an obosan. Go Roshi got rid of him—yet here he is and apparently knowing it all. He's obsessed by food, continually grunting, groaning, smoking, and talking to himself. His breathing (significantly?) is really quite strange. I was sitting in the kitchen doing zazen, basking in the warmth of the wood stove. He was inside, laughing away good-o to himself. "In this Zen, it's marvellous," thinks I, "anywhere else he'd be thought quite mad." Ah, well. His smile is great and he's good about soji. Either way, it's only ten days.

December 13

Shimo's really quite a character, still snorting and adamant over tiny details. He's advanced a lot in koans and I can see why. He has the talent of losing himself totally in what he's doing. He still has a very sharp ego but that only proves to me how much of an ego I still have. If I didn't, I wouldn't be bothered protesting when he insists I do something I know is unorthodox. However. . . .

I could have punched him out last night when we went to Sasaki-san's. That dear old woman is always giving us food and help, so much so that I'm embarrassed to go down with him. He goes down (she's busy, but he plunks us there anyway), and the first thing he says is "Obachan, there are no flowers in Kannonji," with a big peal of laughter from him. She is mortified, apologizing, explaining the price of flowers, the price of the train, wringing her hands, telling him to ask Jakuda-san, not her. She keeps bringing up the subject, obviously disturbed. She tries to tell him some story about the temple; he's only laughing insanely, she shrieking "Listen to me, listen to me." In desperation she tells me the tale. I pretend to understand. She gets out her precious goeka instruments, is playing us a tune. It's beautiful, the expression on her face, mellow, intent, holy. He laughs, halfway through, "We have no more time; must go." For a fraction of a second she looks crestfallen, quickly recovers, finishes her tune through his departure noises, and then she mutters on again about the flowers.

DECEMBER 14

For the last two days I've been able to enter a shallow samadhi. The exciting part is that I have some measure of control over it. As Sekida [in *Zen Training*] has pointed out, it's fundamentally connected with breathing and posture, though his exact methods don't work for me.

Today I feel rotten. For the first time I feel like quitting. Other times I've felt like leaving, but always in the future at a definite date. Now, because the future has no definite date, I just feel like leaving. I won't, of course. I know it's only a mood, and it's quite obvious what's brought this mood to a head. Last night Tessan-san was to phone for takuhatsu information. I left the information and went to the *onsen [hot springs]* with Tachibana Sensei. It happened so quickly I hadn't a chance to think, but about two miles down the road I regretted going. Sure enough, Tessan-san was annoyed that I wasn't there. Knowing that threw me into a kind of wretched mood—totally stupid, the kind of thing I thought I had gotten over. I thought things no longer disturbed me, or at least, only affected me on the outside. Nonsense, another disillusionment. Every time I think I've progressed, I seem to mess it up again.

I volunteered for, insisted on, takuhatsu. Now it seems so ominous. They predict this year to be very severe weather; this time no gloves. It's been nice sleeping in the living room while Shimo's gone. When I'm feeling down, I try to cheer myself up with little perks like that. It would be nice to have someone I could talk with. I don't actually feel lonely but do enjoy company betimes. Before, I always used to console myself with the thought "Ah, well, it's good for me." And it is, yet I feel I could live a more natural life in the West and still continue training. Bah, I know this is just a mood. It's infuriating to be such a victim to moods.

DECEMBER 15

Such a day as yesterday I wouldn't like to go through again in a hurry. My mind was in such a whirl and confusion it's hard even to recollect my thoughts.

I hated him [Shimo] for a thousand little, insignificant things. The fact that they were trivial and insignificant made me hate myself. One year of ascetic practice and I seem to have got nowhere. I sliced through my finger, through the nail; the tip was held on by a sinew. He grudgingly bandaged it, asked nothing about how it felt, only grumbled about my not watching the fire. I felt vaguely hysterical. Did I need stitches? Would I be fingertip-less? Hating him was only a projection of my mind. What blackness was there was in my mind. I lay on the floor, cold, tired, still pumping blood, the room so smoky my eyes stung, and I cried. For a long time.

Tachibana Sensei phoned; he was alarmed to hear my voice. He took me to Morioka. The poor man didn't know quite what to do with the sobbing female but was wonderful. Just to unburden myself, to have someone, anyone, to talk to. We drank coffee between philodendrons, his eyes heavy with concern. "There, there, it only proves you're human. Human relations are important." It was a combination, I guess, hating Shimo and his bossiness made me unduly upset at having angered Tessan-san (by missing his call), my finger, the oppressive greyness of the weather, shoveling snow. . . . I felt trapped for months in the cold, and was secretly dreading takuhatsu.

DECEMBER 20

On the 15th I looked at the calendar and could scarcely imagine lasting the five days until he left; the first five had seemed eternal. He even spoiled the thought of returning to Toshoji, for there I would be with him again. I comforted myself, trying to see the bright side—like the fact that I could sleep in the living room. Big thrill.

But he left yesterday and by then all had changed. I knew it was my mind's projection. We talked; he drank sake, his face turning red by the fire. He never offered me, the guest, any, but it didn't matter. I couldn't understand most of what he said, but that didn't matter either. The warmth was there between us. He said I seemed an extraordinarily happy person. That made me laugh and laugh, having tormented myself so over the last few days. He was earthy. He showed me innocently how to work, to throw oneself wholehearted-ly into one's work. (I'm practising Dokusan with some minor successes). More than any koan, he was a living koan, singing and hearty.

Me and my day of sobbing was all only mood. Now it's gone, released. The pressure of the resentment I felt towards him was checked from anger, so flowed down in tears. Yet it was so encompassing—my very being. All the while I knew it was my own creation, that I was free to rid myself of it, but I couldn't. I, me, my ego-self, was the mood; now it's over and that self is over. The "I" constantly mutates. It has no "essence." Yesterday, alone, I felt very happy, very at peace. "What is it that I lack?" Nothing, absolutely nothing. But that is equally a mood. Because it is more pleasant, I would like to see it as somehow more real, truer, always there behind, but in the same way it will come and go.

Things are resolving themselves nicely. I wanted eggs—expensive, I won't. Then Chiba-san brought them. Tessan-san told me to buy *geta [wooden platform sandals]*; Chiba-san says that for a New Year's present she wants to give me geta. I dreaded no longer sleeping in the living room when Shimo comes back, but realized that if I sleep in the little room I can easily warm it. That was a real weight off my mind, one of my greatest sufferings (amn't I weak?). So I feel sure that takuhatsu will be grand. The dread is gone. The trapped-by-winter feeling is gone. I don't mind at all doing all the work by myself. I'm surprised. Soji just doesn't bother me any more, and I feel no urge to skip or shortcut. I have things organized now; there's time for the temple and for me.

Eshin-san wrote again, a beautiful letter. His love is so pure, sincere, and loyal, much truer than I deserve. In my reply I told him about Killian. It only seemed right. Not that Killian is by any means "the man," but I still do not feel committed.

DECEMBER 22

Still alone and happy. Winter is very much here. In the mornings, getting up at 3:25, it's extremely cold. During the first few days and leading up to the 14th, I strongly resisted the idea of winter. I felt trapped, fed myself lines like "this is the last winter," "Tekkan-san and Kas'ko-san managed," "Only four months," etc. None particularly helpful. Now, strangely, it's changed (not through any heroic efforts of mine.)

In the morning, delivering *buppan [little rice offerings placed before Buddha statues]* at 4:30, I warm my feet on the cooker afterwards, hands like clubs; the same during ookyo. It stings to touch the metal door handles; the buppan are frozen. These days I feel cold, but that's all. There's no comment; my self isn't resisting it nor having to persuade it. Like the koan about not getting wet, I'm cold; of course, I'm cold, but not really cold. Takuhatsu will be fine, and I've wasted so much energy worrying about winter.

KANNONJI, IWATEKEN
DECEMBER 26, 1980

Dear Mum, Scott, Beth, and Jane,

Hard to imagine that you're basking now in Florida sunshine as I look at the falling snow. How was your Christmas this year— beaches and coconuts? Probably as different from our Park Avenue ones as my one was. (Somehow Park Avenue always seems like it was really Christmas.) I have been minding the temple alone of late until the beginning of next month, when a bunch arrive up from Tokyo to beg. The first couple of days seemed a bit lonely, but when I felt a little lonesome I made myself go do some cleaning, and then I was fine. Now I really like having the place to myself—perfect peace and quiet, no one bossing me around, I can do things at my own pace.

Christmas Eve we had a small blizzard. At the start of the blizzard, I took off into the woods, not to be daunted from my celebration, and lopped off the top of a little pine tree. Between the prints of two celestially borne Buddhas, on top of the telephone table, I set up my tree. Trimmed it with old bits of ribbon and some "things" I cooked. No oven of course, so I deep fried and frosted some things with a texture reminiscent of doughnuts and a shape like Christmas balls. (I tried stars, it took all my trigonometry to cut out a pattern for one, but I guess I never got far enough in physics, 'cuz damned if they'd keep their shape. So much for Christmas and higher education.)

Meanwhile, the snow got more insistent. I was doing evensong—the introduction "Dai hi shin dharani" is followed by an impressive drum crashing. Right on cue as I thumped the drum, the power failed. I finished evensong squinting in the twilight, then whipped a candle off the altar and hightailed it back to the kitchen.

I stoked up my fire, sat down to watch the snow fall by candlelight. It was very quiet and peaceful. It had the "peace on earth, good will to all" quality that Christmas should have. All that was missing was you guys, but you were in my mind. Not able to read or do much of anything, with no light I settled down to meditate for a while.

Hardly had I tucked up into a lotus, when Tachibana Sensei burst in like Santa himself, bearing a bag of goodies. Behind him his two sons, like Santa's little elves, came bumbling in ready to tuck into a feast. Tachibana Sensei, bless his heart, brought not only crackers and sweets but a little naggin of whiskey (for the cold, of course) and a Gateaux "Molly O'Rourke" fruit cake. I was stupefied, made right in Dublin. Someone had given it to him five years ago and he'd never touched it. (Must have known a Dubliner would be around for Christmas sooner or later.) I was a bit wary of it, Gateaux cakes at their freshest can often taste like they're five years old. Didn't know how this would be, but time cures all ills (or something). It wasn't just good, but the best fruit cake I've ever had. Must have been the whiskey. Cake with a vintage!

So we sat round the stove in the winking candlelight, chatting and laughing. The kids were delighted at the Christmas tree; it looked better in the low lighting of a one-watt candle.

Christmas morning after breakfast I sat down (with another slice of fruitcake) to open my presies. Thank you. Bethie, I opened yours first, as I could guess what it was, and I played it while opening the rest. A very nice choice of music, it made me feel like I was back at home. I was dying to dive right into the book, Mum, looks *great, not only Rome, D.C., and Korea, but the hero spent part of his childhood in Dublin. I've heard it's very good and someone else said I really should read it. Thanks. I hadn't the chance to sit down for a good read, as I had people coming for a ceremony and a heck of a lot of Christmas Eve blizzard to remove before that. It was the first ceremony I've done alone, but it went well. Christmas was a spectacularly gorgeous day — blue skies, virgin snow, and that savage piercing winter sun that transforms everything to crystal.*

Last night I was exhausted and ready to call it a day early. Didn't feel much like cooking, so my Christmas dinner was a simple rice gruel and piece of tofu. At least no worries about Christmas calories! (Actually it was very tasty.) Did you have all kinds of tropical treats? I suppose you ate out, hope it was good. Takes all the work out of Christmas, leaving all the fun bits, I hope.

LATER

Well, got in my western Christmas-cheer bit after all. A bunch of the Morioka gaijins got together for some traditional fun. Had a bonfire, sung carols in the snow (snowballs and all). For dinner everyone brought a dish. We were American, Irish, English, Afghani, Iranian, and Indian (no Japanese at all!) so the dinner, far from turkey and ham, was very exotic, but finished by mince pies. We all regressed, as we reverted back to childhood memories and party games—even pin the nose on Santa. Great fun altogether.

I'm dying to hear about your Florida festivities. My love to the Sweeneys when you see them. It'll be great having a holiday with them. Richard, who gave last night's party, says he'll make some tapes for me. Thanks for the blanks and the vitamins; they'll be good to keep me fit for begging. I've been holding onto this, hoping to hear from you, but no news. Hope that means you're having an excellent time. I'll pop this off (and probably hear from you immediately).

Love you all dearly, M.

P.S. To Scott and Beth, my heartiest congratulations on your report cards. Those were excellent grades, but even more important than the grades themselves was how they pleased Nana. She wrote telling me how proud of you she was. Making her happy is even better than being top of the class. Anyway I'm proud of you both, too (but don't get swelled heads or I'll bash 'em down). Love yis.

DECEMBER 27

I told Tachibana Sensei about Eshin-san's proposal. His reaction was shocking. It almost frightens me, the suddenness and depth of emotion with which the Japanese can respond. You feel you're always sitting on a potential explosion. He talked nonstop for two hours, carried away, repeating himself, then recovering himself. Eshin-san shouldn't be allowed back. The hara-kiri mentality—He explained he was of the old school, but . . . I was a bit shocked at the end of the session. I was afraid ever to have anything to do with Eshin. Mentally I prepared to write him a letter of rejection. The next evening he phoned.

He declared his love, sounded as if he were reading lines from a play, though I'm sure he's sincere. When he hung up, tears came into my eyes. Why? After talking to Tachibana Sensei, I'm worried about his coming back.

Christmas Eve I was a little lonely at the edges, so I packed myself off to do soji. It worked. Then I lopped off the top of a pine tree during the blizzard and covered it with colored ribbon, then deep-fried overiced "things." The electric power failed. Dinner was by candlelight—gruel and cabbage. Watching the snow fall, so soft and firm like a mother patting her baby to sleep, by the gentle glow of a single candle, I felt quite still and at one, in peace with the world. No Christmas Eve celebrations, and it didn't matter. The lights were out, so I settled down to meditate by the wood stove. Tachibana Sensei burst in like Santa, bearing a bag of goodies. Behind him, his boys tumbled in like elves. He brought a naggin of whiskey and the best fruit cake I've ever had, made right in dear dirty Dublin and enjoyed in Japan. Looking out the window, the candle seemed to glow inside me, but the wood fire seemed to crackle from inside, too. Felt so happy, so simple.

Christmas Day saw loads of snow to shovel and a little unwrapping ceremony while I had my fruitcake breakfast. It made it seem as if the family were here. The day was too sparklingly, spectacularly beautiful to feel homesick or lonely. The sun, dazzling on the virgin white, was elating. In the morning I did my first ceremony alone; it went well. The rest of the day no one came around. Christmas dinner was tofu and rice gruel. Very delicious. No complaints.

Being alone these days, I can work at my own pace. The division between work and rest seems not as sharp and, interestingly, I get flashes wherein time actually feels subjectively different—where it is now totally, not overshadowed by other. Never realized before how very "not-now" my ordinary consciousness is.

Two gaijins are coming for the takuhatsu and Tessan-san will do tenzo. Wasn't I daft to have been worrying? And isn't life grand?

JANUARY 6, 1981

Takuhatsu has begun. I'm tired, but it's okay. Last year I could only survive by promising myself never again. Now it hurts just as much, but it's as if it doesn't matter. I feel I could go on and on. I'm working hard. In the morning I do buppan or *chokka (ino) [morning prayers]*, walk for three hours, rest a half hour, then soji, practice ookyo at 3, at 3:30 collect buppan, at 4:00 do *banka [evensong]*, then every second day I cook. Up in the morning at 3:30 for zazen; evening, too.

Shozan-san has left. Tessan tortured him. He was slow, slow of wit and body, but quick to laugh and share a biscuit. He was always apologizing, grovelling, smiling. He used to be a taxi driver; it shows in his servile manner. Tessan grew impatient, wanted to teach him, and the only way he knew how was by shouting. He picked him up on any little thing, roaring, swiping, even throwing a soup bowl at his head. He left, driven away. Then a poor innocent came who'd never done zazen. He wanted to stay a while. Each took turns exercising ego at his expense. He lasted a night and a day. It was interesting to see how Tessan's relationship with us depended so much on having a release. Shozan-san was his fall guy, and we were marvellous. Shozan left and he laid into us. Shimo-san came, and the foreigners became excellent, whereas Shimo was crazy. But he'd hold his own in a fight. The first night they roared at each other (the night the innocent newcomer came for his first taste of the monastic ideal). Tessan-san seemed pleased—an ally in his camp. Together they bitched about Tessan, and it provided release, but Tessan-san missed Paul and Galli-san. "At least they were normal," said he.

We did have fun with them here. The western youth in me that lies dormant so much of the time in this male, Oriental temple life came out. Galli-san whipped tuneless, heartfilled songs from the guitar; I played the spoons. (Paul composed one about Maura of the mountains and a great one about "I hate takuhatsu, I hate the snow, going back to Tokyo.") After Shimo came, Tess' reaction was to go mute, hang his head, and be as surly as possible. At first he maintained his pleasant disposition towards me, but after a while, during the day, that disappeared too. He wouldn't answer my greetings, made huge fusses about nothing. There were periods, then, when he had to take out his frustrations on me, and he'd blow his top over trivia, especially if I did something like give Tess a cup of tea at an inappropriate time (i.e., anytime). But at least I could understand that it wasn't really me, that he just needed a release. Usually it was grand, though at times I, too, needed a release and cried. It was all so obvious, one bouncing off the other, none with real control, a series of moods, pressures, and repercussions squeezing back and forth in a box. (But at night he usually became charming again.)

Tess did carry *kanshugyo [practice in the cold]* to extremes at times. He wasn't doing it himself, admitted he disliked it. (One of his favorite lines to me when anybody made a mistake but I was to be blamed was "You wanted to do takuhatsu; you wanted to." Although I had never complained, it seemed a fixation to him.) Food would be hidden away. He'd stop me from cooking anything vaguely interesting. Tessaisan was suffering from acute war pains but would sit freezing in his room rather than come in to Tessan's company. I really had to beg Tessan and use all my influence to get him to let Tessai-san use a heater (paying for the oil himself).

Meanwhile, Tessan slept in the warmest room in the house, snuggled into the *kotatsu [a quilt-covered foot warmer]*.

As for us taking turns at tenzo, he did take advantage. His errands were always on my days off, and several times he just plain told me to do his turn. I didn't really mind, though. It's better training the more I have to do. (Bed by 9:30, up at 3:30 to do zazen). But although I didn't mind the work, at times his bitching got to me, and I must admit that when the backbiting started, while I didn't really join in, I also didn't try to bring about reconciliation. That was wrong of me. I feel it strongly. Ultimately, in a situation, it all doesn't matter. Whether we criticize or praise, it all passes, it's all empty, all phenomenal, so I might as well try to make peace in those situations. I, too, was just reacting to situations—or rather the tentative "I" is merely a reaction to different events. All during kanshugyo I was very aware of the passing, phenomenality of circumstances and people. It was so obvious and made everything easy.

Truly this takuhatsu seemed to go fast and was not hard, yet my frostbite was terrible, bleeding and oozing pus. (Though I could have worn gloves, I only did so on a couple of excruciating occasions.) My room was freezing (no heat). Paul came in and was really shocked by its size and temperature. (What with my head in the closet and my feet at the door . . .) Working most of the time, just no problem.

Last year, however, I suffered more. Trying, subjectively, to recall, it seems as if I had more highs off takuhatsu last year. This time it was just something I did and got on with it. There were some lovely moments, though. Sometimes you could actually feel an energy of givingness and purity from the people, and I'd feed off it, feel it surging through me, my voice becoming loud and untiring. Sometimes after *tenjin [a refreshment after takuhatsu]*, sitting by the altar, soft candles glowing and warm welcoming home, having done *choka [morning sutras]* before dawn and walked, roaring, all morning, then offering ookyo again, a wonderful peace seemed to pervade. I was not only here and now, but the whole universe was, and stopped. Everything was very, very still. (Often in the distance, especially when we'd come home, I'd hear sutra-chanting—usually *"Namu ki e butsu."* *["I take refuge in the Buddha."]* Strange, as we weren't chanting that. And one time I heard the Kanzeon Sutra with Paul's voice; mild hallucinations.)

Then, on several occasions during our breaks, people gave us tea and senbei, toast, okashi, or pastries. Oh, but they tasted good! Incredible. I wished I could always appreciate each bite, each sip, with such relish. At times I felt guilty—all these people giving, giving. Little old ladies running after us in the snow, people stopping their cars, young children on their way to school, workers on the upper stories throwing money out the windows, giggling. And why? So we can live. They'll never come here, never be refreshed by the peace of Kannonji, by a good sitting in a quiet zendo. They're all so unselfishly giving only so that I can carry on my practice. I owe them a debt, the debt of my self-oriented (though there is no self!) practice. It's a huge debt, one I'm inclined to shirk.

I got a cat, Gion-chan. At first I felt like a new father being handed twins, awkwardly holding them—"Now what?" But she's lovely. She rides on my shoulder while I cook and keeps me warm at night. Sometimes she's obnoxious.

Tetsugen-san wrote me three letters and sent two parcels. He comes on the 8th. I think it will be good. One of the ladies said my complexion has changed. Tachibana Sensei says I look younger and seem stronger. I think I only look plumper from eating loads of sweet mochi rice cakes. Tessaisan, because of his dislike of Tessan, was inclined to exaggerate the extent to which I've been working, so now everyone thinks I virtually carried takuhatsu. But it's not so. I worked, but not very much more than usual. It just was no problem.

JANUARY 8

I realize how easily people are fooled in spiritual affairs. They want to believe people have attained depths and to feel associated with the extraordinary. At Jakuda-san's, after dokusan, a new woman was seated with us on the floor around the kerosene stove. They were all devout old women, religion the most important issue in their lives. Transposing cultures, if I were with these same kind of women in my own Ireland, I'd represent the antithesis of all they devote their lives to. Here, in a culture totally foreign to my old one, I not only sympathize with them but am even more involved (fanatical?) than they. Strange. . . . The new woman asked questions about me, and they began talking about me, not telling untruths, but the things they selected to point out made me seem special, deep—even the shine in my eyes. The woman seemed almost infatuated, holding my hand, gazing into my eyes, saying how glad she was to meet me. It made me wonder if there are hundreds of unscrupulous people with as little insight and understanding as me, masquerading as being in some way developed and capable of teaching. Irresponsible.

During takuhatsu I got a letter from Jean-Luc. The first time. I hadn't heard from him in almost a year. I dreamt he came to Kate's wedding; the next day this letter arrived. I was thinking how I'd made a bit of a fool of myself writing five postcards but with so little response. I sent him a Christmas card; he didn't answer. Then next day, this letter. Lovely. He's very interested in Zen, wants to be my student in Zen. He signed beautifully in English, Spanish, and French. I allowed myself the luxury of daydreaming about him a bit. He's spending next month with his girlfriend.

Many times during the past year I wondered if I wasn't somehow missing out, vaguely feeling that by the time I re-entered my old world everyone would have settled into couples. Those feelings aren't there anymore, partly from having gone home when I did, partly from feeling there will always be men, and partly from not caring whether there are or not. It just doesn't seem to occupy my mind. I suppose now that I've said that, it will become an obsession. It seems as soon as

I recognize any change or progress, its opposite makes itself apparent.

Tetsugen-san arrived and seems gentle and undemanding, helpful and appreciative. He has a quiet nature that is at times tinged with sadness but he is usually smiling. His kidney has been removed, and twice a week all his blood has to be cleaned by machine. He has been practising for ten years and seems to me to be much more of a true priest than Tessan or Shimo. He has no need to assert himself egotistically. In fact, he is perhaps too humble, saying that he's disappointed with his progress so far.

I didn't realize quite how basic Tessan-san's and my life here were until Tetsugen-san came. Even in the depths of the northern winter, we didn't use a heater and only lit the wood stove a couple of hours a day. I was used to doing breakfast and buppan with numb fingers in temperatures of -9°C. I couldn't believe it when he offered me a stove for my room. (However, I refused.) He even buys food. For months now we've been surviving on a basic diet of *daikon [Japanese radish]*, cabbage, and rice. Tessan-san didn't want to use even brown rice, because it took an extra five minutes of gas to cook and that was a waste. There are little things, like the fact that now we don't have to keep boiling the same tea leaves all day, so they were only bitter. I used nearly to blind my eyes trying to make out the tiny *hiragana [phonetic Japanese characters]* in the morning dimness; now we can use a light.

161

Yet Tessan-san provided a good training, for now I really don't care one way or the other about such things.

JANUARY 12

I feel very glad to be young, not just mentally (as I sometimes feel) but physically. After shovelling snow in the sunshine, my body felt strong, straight, and young. It was wonderful striding through the snow, shovel on my shoulder, breeze in my hair.

JANUARY 15

Buddha's *inaku naru day [the day Buddha entered Parinirvana, left this world]*. I tried doing zazen all night. Very cold. Not very good.

JANUARY 16

I'm amazingly untired. All day and when I'm falling asleep a voice resounds in my head, "I am empty, I am impermanent." There's a peace about this voice; it keeps other noisy thoughts from entering.

After his trip to the hospital, Tetsugen's arm always hurts, though he says that otherwise it's not really painful. When he comes back he looks weak and drained. Often he looks grey. His eyes are close together, so from the side they're scarcely visible. He stares into space and seems colourless, eyeless, lifeless. Other times, he's full of energy but talks little. He's very good to Gion-chan, who lately has been driving me bats. She's been bringing out the worst in me, so I imagine what it would be like to be re-born as a cat and try to treat Gion as I'd want to be treated.

We're having a spring thaw. Beautiful—a black old man pushing a black barrow, etched against the wintry fields. The mountains breathing greys, blacks, whites in mists of *sumi-e* [ink] paintings. Coming home in the dusk from the onsen, I wanted never to stop. . . .

Kannonji, Iawateken
January 26, 1981

Dear Mum, Scott, and Beth,

Glad to hear you enjoyed your holiday. Lucky divils. Sounds like you finally got the Christmas you've been wanting, Mum. Scott, how was your birthday? What did you do to celebrate? If you took any pictures, I'd love copies. Any more good ones of the weddings? I thought the photos in the paper were good, though not Geoff's best angle. Beth, how are your rabbits? I got a new kitty; she's all black and full of mischief, and I'm mad about her. (She's sitting on my lap right now trying to capture my pen.) She keeps me lovely and warm at night. I gave Mu-chan your letter, Wiggs. She was very pleased, but it took her three days with a dictionary to read it. She promised that she'll answer you, but she may be slow. She wants to go to school in Ireland and wishes you'd come to Japan so that she could meet you.

Back here, begging has started, and the temple's been like a 3-ring circus. Of the people who came for begging, two have run away completely from monastic life, and two returned early to Tokyo. That leaves me with three very strong-willed monks that don't get along with one another. It can be like treading on eggshells. Each one takes turns being wonderful to me as I am the neutral party—or should I say "referee." But so much tension builds up that at times I get my head blown off for no reason, so I keep a low profile. It's pretty comical, really, and at times it's hard to keep a straight face. After all my worrying about the cold when begging, it turned out quite grand this year. The clothes are a big help, but even at that I must be more used to it or something, because my hands are still bare and frostbitten yet the whole thing doesn't take anything out of me this time . . . a pleasant surprise and relief. I've been on television again, three times, local and national. Mum, I'm sure you were disappointed by the videotape of the program that I sent you, but they shot for a day and a half and from that cut out all except the image they wanted to create. They chose to edit out everything about you guys, my studies at Trinity, and my "bourgeois" background. They had an idea of the poor little monk that they wanted to push, hence the shots of my room and my tatty sandals. . . . There have been quite a few lunches out during begging. The local people put on these wonderful spreads. This time I've been taking notes and asking for recipes, so next time I see you guys I'll make a big Japanese feast. Meals here at the temple are mostly cabbage, daikon, and rice. Any good recipes?

Much love, M.

Kannonji, Iwateken
February 12, 1981

Dear Nana,

Happy Valentine's Day and happy spring. I hope the winter so far hasn't been too harsh for you. Here we're just finishing "daikan," the great cold. Yesterday we had mamemaki [bean throwing], *something akin to Halloween in so far as it is a day for driving out evil spirits. Everyone throws beans and peanuts, shouting to scare out whatever evil may lie in store for the new year. Then we had a big party. Go-Roshi, the teacher, was up from Tokyo, and all his students came. It was great fun, as everyone helped out—but we'll be eating leftover seaweed rolls for weeks! There is a new monk*

*coming to stay here next week. He has been training in the temple
on this card [Sojiji] for four years. Seems amiable. All my best wishes. Be careful of the flu.*

Love, Maura

MARCH 7

Galli-san has come and gone. He was meant to stay
two or three days but gradually it extended to about two
weeks. We had fun, sheer, innocent, can't-stop-laughing-
over-nothing, really funny fun. He said that in Tokyo he had
been very angry and upset.

We talked a bit about muji. He was suffering the same
way I had from not really understanding what he was trying
to do with it and there was no one he could talk to about it.
I told him just to lose himself in his work, to throw himself
into it, and he is muji expressing itself. This idea he seemed
to grasp for the first time and thus totally. He did a com-
mendable practice, diving in with energy and enthusiasm.
Having spoken with him and seeing his efforts, I was re-
inspired to heed my own words. Our *gaijin ookyo [foreigners'
sutras]* in the morning strained at the rafters. So we did muji
yuki kaki, muji soji, muji dancing—all the while laughing

and throwing snow balls and sipping *umeboshi [plum]* tea. At times we felt sorry for Tetsugen-san. He went through a dark period for a few days, when he scarcely spoke or even answered the most mundane of greetings; meanwhile, we could scarcely restrain our spontaneous mirth. At times it infected even Tetsugen-san, and he giggled. Up on the roofs, we abandoned ourselves to shovelling snow in the sunshine, conquering each new piece of ice, slipping, catching, victoriously detached slides, down, down. . . . Back on the ground, pulling the waste from the outhouse, carrying it in reeking bucketsful to the fields, or building a snowman, walking, singing, to the post office. He was very Italian, emotional, easy to bring up. Poor Jiko-san would watch his hands, waving a mile a minute, like a dizzy puppy or a kitten waiting to spring.

Jim gave a party and we went. Galli threw himself into dancing with the same vigour. He was taking muji very seriously.

He danced on, oblivious to the small clutch of females now gathering around him, subtly dancing for him. I left the room and found another scene—people sitting on the floor, playing guitars, less frenetic, very warm. It only occurs to me now that the same thing happened to me as happened to Galli; a little group of inebriated admirers gathered, fawning. We danced and sang 'til very nearly zazen time. I grabbed a couple of hours sleep but scarcely felt tired.

Jim came to begin my sculpture. We were standing in the chilly corridor, my hands turning shades of blue and purple. He was shocked and insisted on bringing me to the hospital. I was embarrassed—they seemed so much better. The infection had gone inside and was erupting in mounds of pus. I remembered all the mornings when I (like the little match girl!) clawed at the twigs, my hands red and oozing, trying to shake off the snow from the sticks so that they'd light. I realized I must have been carrying an infection for two months. They gave me an antibiotic, and it's nearly gone in just a week.

I went to dokusan. I had to repeat the koan about "All this universal law is like a dream, a vision, foam, shadow, dew, thunder. This you must realize." I did a mirage; he didn't understand. For my foam, Go Roshi burst into laughter as I blew it. For shadow, he loped around, trying to kill his shadow. (I had merely sat still, one hand following another.) For dew, he hiked up his robes, stalked through the fields, heaved a heavy stone to find himself drenched. (My dew had disappeared with the sun. I'm still too intellectual.) For thunder, he banged and tumbled to the ground. For "this you must realize," he said I must roar it, thumping my leg. He asked for the meaning. Originally, I had explained that it was all my daily activities, but I thought he felt this was wrong. So this time I said I was empty and impermanent. Tachibana Sensei, trying to translate this, looked puzzled. I explained I meant myself and all things. Go Roshi said it was my everyday activities.

He asked me to stay at Kannonji until Tetsugen-san

married. (He used to laugh at that possibility.) And then he'd have me come to Toshoji. Either way is fine with me.

I thought, one day, of my father. I loved him. He lived 43 years, died, and is no more. It made me sad. He was such a wonderful man. No one knows him any more, loves him any more. He can no longer touch any one, move people. Lived, died, and gone like so many hundreds of millions. As I will. Galli-san says he loves my father; for that I love Galli-san. He really had a feeling for him, kept asking about him, reminding me to give him his photo.

"I want to meet your father," he said.

"You can't," I said. "He's dead."

"I will. You will be my father."

Perhaps the reason that I love Galli-san's love of Dad is not so much from my love of him as of my own frail, human shunning of my own mortality. Yet I do not exist. There is nothing to lose.

Dear Mum,

. . . *They say the most pleasant months to visit Japan are
May and December. May would probably be too soon for you.
August isn't nice, and June rains a lot. I'm presuming I can get free
time. As soon as you're definite, I'll ask. Except for sesshin times
(about 5 days a month in summer) I should be able to get some time
off, if I know in advance. I may be here at Kannonji for some time
yet. As I guess I told you, the present monk really can't manage
alone. They're looking for a wife for him. It's so businesslike here.
Until then, I've been asked to stay and help. I gladly accepted.
Spring and summer are so much nicer here than in muggy, big city
Tokyo. Our normal quiet work routine was disrupted for the past ten
days when Galli-san, a hilarious Italian who lives in the dormitory
section of Toshoji came to visit. He's vivacious and animated, also a
big help. The poor little mute monk here didn't know what to make
of him but had to giggle. So the temple mood was decidedly different. Things are always happening here. That was fun, but this peace
is also wonderful. The only sounds are the birds calling and the
dripping of the melting snow (though actually we can usually hear
the nearby highway). Next month we'll have the first sesshin of the
year. I'm looking forward to it. They're like a transfusion and I can*

make progress on my koans. Now that you're reading so much about
Zen, these terms probably make sense. Have you heard of the
Mumonkan collection of koans? I'm beginning those now. . . .

Lots of love, M.

MARCH 11

Coincidence—I was thinking of how I no longer have
to teach English and was glad. Then I was thinking about
how Chiba-san wanted to learn English once. Just such silly
light thoughts. Then Chiba-san came and asked me to
resume the English lessons.

My zazen is rotten. I read in Dogen Zenji's piece that if
your mind is contemplating Buddhahood and Bodhisattvas,
the deep meaning of the sutras, etc., it's no good. But as soon
as I sit down to meditate, I'm filled with thoughts of what to
cook for dinner. Before my koan comes to mind, it's
thoughts of soup. I know good samadhi concentration is
really important, and I don't seem to be able to concentrate
at all.

Yesterday I spent the day sewing at Sasaki-san's. She's an incredible woman, 70 years old but simply bursting with vitality. She ascribes it to hard work and going to the temple for ookyo at 5:30 each morning. Even through fresh snow she wends her way to Kannonji, bent double across her walking stick from years in the rice paddies. She's always talking excitedly, breathlessly, hands animated, gesticulating, bouncing on her worn legs, cocking her dyed black head flirtatiously—70 years old and irrepressible. While sewing and cutting, she can't suppress the smile flowing from her joy in life. Too frank to play games, she freely "praises herself and chastizes others," all the while laughing and working. The sun streamed in. We sat on the floor, stitching, her wrinkled hands as nimble at the needle as in speech. She wears a thimble like a wedding band. In and out, in and out, in perfect rhythm, every stitch straight and of equal length. She plies me with goodies, says "hurry back," and I scarper through her little oriental garden of pools and rocks and tapered shrubs. I half walk, half skip (she's infectious) past the snow-covered apple orchard with its single black crow on a naked bough, then back to make the lunch and to stretch out with a cup of tea. The mountains look higher, more nebulous. Life is wonderful. Truly, what is it I lack? Nothing. It's so simple.

Jim came. He asked me many questions about Zen and consciousness, etc. I felt reluctant to answer. I knew my explanations could only be shallow and his approach only intellectual. So we talked. It was hard to explain on a level he'd appreciate, which means, of course, that I was intellectualizing, too. He's forming a little *benkyo'o-kai [study group]* for reading and discussion. As he was leaving, he kept saying that he really hoped I'd be able to come. He had obviously found our discussion stimulating.

So, shortly afterwards, as I was walking down the hall where he'd been sculpting, with buppan in my hands, the thought flickered across my mind: "Jim thinks I'm interesting." Then, CRASH, I hit the door with the tray, spilling water (nothing broke) and I suddenly woke up and felt very ashamed. Humiliated. He thought I was interesting because of what I was saying about Zen—bandying about "no-mind" and "emptiness" and the like, and here I was, not only thinking and intellectualizing, but being vain, too. Am so ashamed.

Then there's the cat. She really had been bold of late, dirtying my bed, stealing food, climbing where she knows she's not supposed to. We figured we'd have to train her while she's young, but we just seem to be punishing her too often. She ducks if you move your hands suddenly. She doesn't drive me crazy any more. (I've got used to her shrieking and pouncing on my shoulder when I'm concentrating.) I only punish her when she deserves it—which I still think may be too much. But Tetsugen-san upsets me a bit, because he punishes her cruelly, unnecessarily. He is always jumping at her, teasing and tormenting her, shouting, locking her out. He used to be kind to her, kinder than I. Now she's afraid of him.

Perhaps he feels guilty. He had a dream in which I took her away because he was always getting angry at her. I feel awful. She's here because I like cats, yet she must feel miserable. It's my responsibility.

MARCH 17

I'm disgusted with myself. I'm dawdling in my practice. I'm resolved to get up in the morning promptly, eat less, do four hours of zazen daily, and not stop until I reach complete enlightenment. No more fooling around. I'm trying to work with "What is this mind?" It's teasing and frustrating.

I've been thinking about Dominique [an English girl, teaching in Morioka]. I feel a sense of responsibility towards her. She really wanted to do zazen but has never gotten around to coming. I've told her the bus but never gave her the extra little push of offering to meet her or arranging a time. She was so excited at the possibility. I must arrange a definite time.

Dear Mum,

Happy St. Patrick's Day. Your card arrived today and I wouldn't have known the day but for Beth's nice decoration. . . . Go Roshi gave me a surprise a while ago. You recall my telling you the plan for his daughter, Mariko-san, to marry a priest from Kyushu and then inherit this temple by way of dowry. Temples are passed on in that way. Well, I guess poor Mariko-san didn't like the monk; anyway she refused. So Go Roshi stripped her of the dowry and in dokusan suddenly floors me by saying that if I marry a good Zen man, he'll give me the temple as a wedding present with which to build an international Zen dojo. I was very touched by the offer, after I got over my shock, but had to turn him down. They're so matter-of-fact about marriage here. People are obviously beginning to worry that I'm getting long in the tooth, and they really find it hard to credit that I don't want to get married! By the way, you came into the master plan, Mum, you and any of the kids would be brought here to live and would be taken care of! . . .

Winter is jerkily giving way to spring—can't believe it went so fast. Life has settled to a lovely pace and a peaceful routine. Plenty to do, but not too busy, and things seem so quiet. The air is *fresh and pure off the mountains, smelling of pine trees and spring thaw. The birds are returning and chirping away.*

After I go to sesshin in Tokyo, I'll be going to my first ever Japanese wedding. The second Tessan-san who was here (can you keep track of all the names?) is getting married. The whole thing still is hard for me to conceive of. They've met once. He wasn't even all that impressed, but she wasn't bad, and he liked the temple that came with her and really wanted to get married. So the date was set. As business-like as that. One puts more effort into buying a new car. Strange, then, how well many of these marriages turn out. Perhaps they're not going into them with all sorts of illusions and expectations. Glad to hear that Kate and Geoff sound so happy and are working hard on the new house.

Mum, you said you've been reading about Zen and Japan. What have you been reading, and what do you make of it? I'm very interested. You should practice sitting on the floor, because most people don't have chairs. We have 2 or 3 stowed away somewhere, but for example you couldn't eat, as they're higher than the table. In Japan it's considered polite to sit up properly on the legs, but it hurts most foreigners at first. . . .

Love to you all, M.

Spring Equinox. We go to different houses to chant sutras for their dead for one week around the equinox. I try to really contact them (and Dad) so that perhaps in hearing ookyo they may be liberated. Yet often my concentration fails, and I wonder what's left to call to or to be liberated. What does happen at death? Who am I?

It's lovely going around to the houses, being welcomed in, chanting, chatting, warm and snug in kotatsus, served tea and sweet cakes. Abe-san was chatting animatedly, a soft light behind her through the paper door. Perhaps it was the light, a sort of funeral parlor subtlety, but suddenly it struck me— she will be dead. So alive and vibrant now, then dead and gone. First they'll chant sutra for her and remember, and gradually not even remember as the ripple subsides into the ocean. As we went along through the traffic, all the faces seemed to me to be death masks. . . .

I'm so impressed with these zenkai ladies. There's something in their eyes that dances. I began to wonder if all Japanese were like that (since they are mostly the company I keep), but they aren't. Galli-san noticed it at once as kensho. That was on his mind, but I'm sure he's right.

Jacuda-san was talking. I could only make out a part of what she was saying. She said something about one time in dokusan there was light coming out of Go Roshi. The fact that I couldn't fully understand her was not so important. She held me with her eyes. They didn't seem to blink or flicker but seemed to swallow me up. I felt an intense gratitude towards her. As the head of Morioka zenkai, she has taken care of so many sesshins, made it possible for Go Roshi to give dokusan. I felt not just my own thankfulness but that of every *unsui [monk undergoing Zen training]* she's nourished, every sesshin she's catered for. She mentioned Dogen, and tears began to rise to my eyes. I'm grateful to her, to Dogen, to all the Buddhas and patriarchs. But there was power in her gaze.

MARCH 21

I've been socialized. I don't know how or who did it (I suspect Tessan-san) but now I jump up, get the tea, fetch like a servant or a dog or a Japanese wife. It is a real socialization because I wasn't even aware of it and don't really mind. But thank God I wasn't born here and will never marry a Japanese man. (What am I saying? Never marry. Period.) *Chonans [eldest sons]* are the worst.

I've been re-reading a bit of Freud through the light of Buddhism. It's interesting how his concept of the wish ties in with that of desire, instinct with craving—craving to live, craving to die—theos and eros. This craving leads to a new reincarnation (without soul), like being born with instincts but as yet no personality.

Freud thinks telepathy may be primitive pre-linguistic communication. That makes sense if the universe is really one fabric. Plants, of course, have now been shown to possess consciousness. Why do we say rocks are not alive?

Dominique came. She cycled out from Morioka through rain and then sun. Good on her. We talked and talked, 'til I was embarrassed to have talked so much. She's still not sure. One thing that really pierced me somewhere sensitive (we were drying dishes under the dim kitchen light) was when she whirled around and said, "You shouldn't be here. You should be with children, with people, where you can do some good. Look at you. You're radiant. People shouldn't have to cycle miles to see you." And of course I do love children and love people, but I'd hate it if people looked to me when I'm so immature in my practice. I'd hate to fall off. Even to her I spoke too much, saying some things I'd read rather than experienced. I felt ashamed. I told her to forget all I'd said, that I was still shallow. I could see that she took it as false modesty on my part. That night I read in Dogen that he said we shouldn't act like enlightened masters. I felt personally chastized. What can one do? In the koan "the man up the tree" I always felt he must just display his Buddha-nature. That is what Go Roshi does. But what about when it's still so dull?

Funny things have come up in my meditations—daydreams, bad concentration. One idea is to have a Zen commune attached to a monastery so that lay people could also do training, with child care facilities so that terms of 100 days at a time would be possible. Then people could also train at least three years, but if they didn't want always to be monks they could pass on into the commune.

Sesshin. I must do a good one. [Kyogen], my koan, not good. Kyogen is all sounds. But sounds and I are not separate. I am Kyogen.

Now, after sesshin, I had an excellent session. I entered Mumonkan. I made new resolves. I'll try sleeping without lying down, do more soji. On the first night of no sleep, at around 11:00, I felt very tired; around 1:30, my mind became crystal clear; I could only think of my koan. Unfortunately, I guess I overanalyzed it. As I was working with it, I got so involved that it was like a dream. I even had trouble remembering it. I began imputing motives to the people in the koan; they would have been my motives. Go Roshi wasn't impressed. The second night I slept. The third night I slept about two hours sitting up and on the zendo floor. I found my knees ached, so I sat on Go Roshi's step with Mumonkan on my head so I wouldn't fall asleep. (The book on the head is very helpful.)

PART VII

New Resolve

Dear Mum,

 . . . *As I was quietly sitting here minding my own business writing to you, this monk just asked me to marry him. At first I didn't understand. Anything vaguely romantic is so far from the tone of our strictly partnership relationship as to be inconceivable. The Japanese language allows sufficient ambiguity that at first I thought he was talking in the abstract, i.e., would I ever marry someone? I answered with what I thought was appropriate indifference, and by thus not initially refusing outright, I got a whole plot laid before me. He says that Go Roshi had said, if I wanted to marry this monk, it would be fine by him. He presented the proposal, if it could be called that, very practically. As he was sick, he needed a cook and we could continue life pretty much as before. My God, are they businesslike! I was almost too shocked to speak. He offered to support you and any of the kids here and said I could go back to Ireland every so often. I was still speechless and bumbled and stumbled and said I'd write to you. Meanwhile, Go Roshi had told me that he wanted me back in Tokyo, where I could train better with him. He had apologized profusely that I had to mind an "invalid" and promised that by July at the latest I'd be back in Tokyo. He said that if I stayed for the 3* years' course of study (I'm half-way) that then I could go back to Ireland and teach. (I know he'd help finance a dojo.)

I made a lot of progress at this last sesshin (just got back). The monk who was translating for me said that in three days I did as many koans as he in six months! Go Roshi and I work well together and it would be difficult to find someone as good. So here are my options—give me your advice. In the midst of my stumblings with Tetsugen-san, and after he'd said "Well then, it's decided. Let's marry" (At times like that my Japanese seems faulty. What had I said?), I, frantically searching for an out, said there was a boyfriend I still hadn't given up on and wanted to write to. I really hate this constant pressure to marry. Everyone worries that I'm getting old, etc.—it's only meant as kindness. But what I might do is accept this nebulous boyfriend, stay until the end of autumn (that will be two years), then go to France, find another Roshi, and do post-grad work.

The other option is to calm down (I am inclined to bolt terribly when people begin talking about marriage), then go back to Tokyo, finish my term of study properly, i.e., the three years, and get the whole training solidly under my belt. I do risk messing things up by breaking too soon. What do you think? Actually, having written to you I already feel calmer. Big deal—if everybody keeps pushing me to marry I can just refuse. I just get to squirming as if there's a noose there. Tetsugen will get over it; it's not as though he's in love with me or anything. But anyway, what do you think I should do? Try to be objective—not just thinking another year-and-a-half off in Japan, but thinking also about my qualifications for the future. Tell Nana not to worry. There's absolutely no way I'll stay in Japan. Cripes, at this rate they'll drive me out!

Anyway, sorry to have gone on at such length, but he just now sprang it on me. As I said, I'm just back from sesshin in Tokyo. It was excellent; I'd say the best one yet. Toshoji has changed a bit from my days there. Someone found out about the cheap dormitory accommodation they offer to Zen students and advertised it in an English paper so now there are four foreigners, even one woman. It's much less isolating, I should think, than before. One of the foreigners, a Jewish student from Pittsburgh called Paul, is over here doing research on Japanese theatre. He got free tickets for a recital, so I went along. It was fantastic, and the best part was having a guide who could explain the various styles, techniques, and meanings of different gestures. It was called a dance recital, but they also did many pieces from Kabuki and Noh plays. They're marathon performances, starting at 12 noon and going on into the night. People drift in and out when they please. The pieces are unrelated, so they don't miss anything. The audience chats, shouts encouragement, picnics, and generally relaxes, having a good time. Watching them all decked out in magnificent, special occasion kimonos was almost as entertaining as the performance.

The other highlight of my Tokyo sojourn was going to Tessan-san's marriage ceremony. It was my first wedding here and unusual in being Buddhist. Weddings are usually Shinto. They had only met a couple of times before the wedding, yet both were cool as cucumbers about it. She looked gorgeous, serene and radiant, as she sat waiting on a throne. Her head was covered by a white hood in deference to the superstition that women have horns! Her first outfit was white silk; then she changed several times, the number of changes being an indication of the wealth of the family. Poor girl, though—she had so many layers on she could scarcely move and couldn't touch a bite of her dinner. There's another custom which says that no one may mention parting, good-bye, or separation during the day. If they do, it's meant to bring bad luck, and the couple may split up. So everyone drifts away without good-byes.

The actual ceremony is very simple and beautiful (no promises of love!). They used a lacquer set just like yours to serve the bride and groom during the ceremony. Then, with sake poured from exquisitely ornamented gold vessels, we all drank to their health and prosperity. After the ceremony, a lot of sake flowed with a feast that made our weddings look like Saturday night's reheated leftovers. It was sumptuous (cost about $80.00 a head), and they even weighed us each down with presents as we left. As they were getting ready to go off to Kyushu on their honeymoon, they looked a funny pair. He wore western clothes instead of his monk's outfit. Having no hair with his navy-blue suit made him look a bit like a con-man; she with her tight, prim little suit could easily have been the social worker turned warden. We all went as far as Tokyo on the train together. The newlyweds sat in separate compartments without even a pretense of romance. Thank God I'm not Japanese.

So now I'm back here at Kannonji. I've just been out digging my vegetable patch, and there's great satisfaction in getting all the preparations done. I've calmed down a bit since my proposal. I'm sure Go Roshi did not suggest it, which is the impression Tetsugen-san was trying to give. Go Roshi always says he wants me back in Tokyo, where I can train more intensively. . . . See you soon.

Much much love, M.

APRIL 20

A bit of a gap. Let's see now. I stayed in Tokyo until the 10th. It was a wonderful time. Sesshin was excellent. There were no major kensho-type breakthroughs, but several nice little "Ah, so desu ka" jerks. Go Roshi asked me to stay in

Kannonji until July at the latest, then back to Toshoji. He says if I want to marry Tetsurai-san, that's okay. I wish he'd drop the marriage thing.

Yesterday a letter from Paul and Galli-san. They said that Eshin-san has become a monk again. He may well fall in love with Sochun-san. She's marvellous, like spring sunshine after a bleak winter. She's always laughing, always bustling around working, overflowing with joy and energy. I was very touched when she wrote me a lovely letter saying how I had inspired her. If only she knew how she had inspired me. She could teach me much about true Zen practice. All during sesshin and the days that followed there was an uplifting sense of *sangha [community, congregation]*. It's something I miss here. The crazy gaijin and Yokokawa-san, with her huge sensitive eyes and poetry, and Jiko-san, as daft as ever, racing down the train platform, holding the carriage. They're wonderful.

Paul-san took me to a Japanese dance performance. I saw my first bit of live traditional Japanese culture and had my first *obento [lunch in a box]*. I've only been here one-and-a-half years! Paul couldn't believe it. It was a marathon, beginning at noon and continuing until evening. He explained many things to me. There's Noh, Kabuki, and puppets. Noh came from the Zen mind, he said. It's very simple, with different gestures having pre-ordained meanings, like a language. Pine trees in the background of the stage mean that it used to be performed at Shinto shrines. Kabuki was a reaction to Noh. It's much more flamboyant and fast-moving, almost gaudy. It's often preceded by a striped curtain. Kabuki is a family monopoly. A few families get all the lead roles. They don't allow women, so a boy is trained from childhood to be an *onnagata [female impersonator]*. Japanese dancers usually have a repertoire of about one hundred pieces, any of which they'll do at two minutes' notice. So rehearsals are few (same pieces, over and over). If one's mother is sick, one can cancel at a moment's notice; it's not like the cutthroat competition in the American theater world.

The audience was fun to watch. In the afternoon it was mostly old ladies, elegantly clad in their silk kimonos. It was like a picnic; people ate, drank, chatted, shouted encouragement to the cast. Occasionally, a pair of hands could be seen moving with it, obviously a dancer who knew that piece. By our standards, it could scarcely be called dance, just movement. The women were totally constrained in their girdle-like layers of kimonos. They kept changing costumes on stage with the help of little men dressed in black that the audience literally didn't see.

One day, Jim took me to a fancy hotel. We drank endless cups of coffee, watched the bureaucrats dressed to match each other, and the decor, in tasteful, subtle, banal non-colours. Then we slowly meandered through the galleries, poking through the streets of downtown Tokyo. I really felt like a country bumpkin who'd come up to the big city. Everything was exciting, a thrill. I could scarcely contain myself.

All during that sesshin, I felt a joy bordering on ecstasy, a huge love for everyone around me. I could scarcely keep from smiling. There was an affinity with everyone, people with whom I'd never even spoken. When someone would have kensho, it was I that felt relieved. Sitting in the corridor, the young lad beside me heaved great tortured "mu's." Each one went through me, until tears dripped down my face with his anguish. This sense of sangha that I said I lack in Kannonji was not at all from need. I can manage quite well, peacefully alone. But it was rather from love. All this love welling up inside was begging for an object. I ask myself, why can't Tetsugen-san be my object? He is there. But with the language barrier and his inhibited personality, it is difficult to have a real relationship, and intimacy is hard even to imagine. But he is good and kind to me, though in other moods he is bossy and demanding. Tachibana Sensei says he treats me as a thing, a temple attachment, but that is only his manner, not his heart.

When I came back from Tokyo he asked me to marry him. I thought he was speaking of marriage in the abstract and said either way was okay. He said it was the same for him, so we might as well marry! I was aghast. He was practical. He needed someone to cook, clean, etc. His sickness pension would provide. It was all so calculated. He ran down my benefits in the contract—I could occasionally return to Ireland, he'd support my mother, etc. My stomach was turning, my mind racing. I began not to understand Japanese, and I thought I was postponing the decision, when he triumphantly exclaimed "So, then, it's decided. We'll marry." I gulped, then backtracked frantically, trying not to hurt his feelings, forgetting that feelings weren't really part of the offer. Since I happened to be in the middle of writing a letter to Mum, I stalled, saying I'd ask her.

The next few days, I felt claustrophobic. He was charming to me most of the time and a cruel bastard to the cat, tormenting her, hitting her, locking her up, inventing nasty teasing games of intimidation. I'd look at him and feel blackness. When I found her locked overnight in Busshari-to, I wanted to scream at him. How could I ever marry a man who'd be so cruel to a cat? The blackness was in my heart. Where was my lofty love for mankind? I felt trapped. What he did physically to the cat I felt emotionally as me (maybe I overreacted). I resented that he could dare to think of dooming me to the banal existence I'd have with him, he who had scarcely enough life in him to look people in their eyes. But surely I should be indifferent. If I really just took a day at a time, then anyone, anywhere, any life should surely be okay. I pelted myself with recriminations. I wanted to run. Any excuse. Aagh. Then a letter came from Mum. She still hadn't received mine, but I used it as an opportunity to make my refusal plain. He took it well. After all, he had little emotion invested in the whole thing. I was amazed at how relieved I felt—amazed and vaguely shocked. Get your act together, kid!

Dear Mum,

Happy birthday to you. Omedeto gozaimasu. Tanoshi tanjoobi da to ii desu ga. A wee package is on the way but will be late. Gomen nasai, ne? [Sorry!] You'd better blinking well make it over to Japan. As soon as you have a definite date, please tell me. I'm still assuming that I'll be able to get free time, though if I'm in Toshoji, as is the plan, it should be easier. Go Roshi is coming here to stay for a while in May. I'm looking forward to it so I can advance with my koans. You're right that Nana seems to think I'm getting too involved. I got a come-back-home but very nice letter from her. . . .

By now you must have gotten my last letter with my almost hysterical reaction to Tetsugen-san's proposal. Poor fellow. I did calm down, and he wasn't at all put out that I wasn't interested. I was amazed at my almost allergic reaction to the mention of marriage. . . .

I went the other day with Mu-chan's mother to see the cherry-blossoms. They're lovely. Underneath the trees sit little parties of "Ohanami no hito," people who've gone blossom viewing. You imagine pastoral picnics, quiet family outings with Oriental tranquility. They're mostly mobs of rowdy drunks out with any excuse to

share a bottle of sake and some songs. Still, they look as if they're
enjoying themselves: "Blossoms, what blossoms?" And the Japanese
need these chances to let themselves go. Anyway, m'dear, the very
happiest of birthdays to you. . . .

Love to ya, M.

MAY 4

Tessan-san came with his bride for the night. Though there were times I thought he'd drive me batty, I really do feel a love for him. When he shows his good side, it's like a winter's hearth. The two of them seem to be doing well by each other, both a little chuffed at being married and each aware of rescuing the other from the shrivelled, cobwebby shelf of spinsterhood. They seemed positively playful with one another, she tapping his newspaper. (Why can't the Japanese touch?) They could even have married for love.

Where Christianity preaches original sin, Buddhism preaches original enlightenment.

Yesterday had dokusan. Phew. Go Roshi gave a big speech about how he'd never met a girl as diligent as me (hasn't met many girls in training). About how I was the same calibre as the old priests, the likes of Dogen. (It's more a reflection of the low quality of present-day Japanese priests.) The upshot of the thing is that he wants to make me Kannonji's *jushoku [head priest]*. I nearly died. Wants to get Tetsurai-san all trained (provided he doesn't run away) and then marry us! Leps. I glugged.

He said only my children were fit to be successors of Kannonji, and though he had looked all over Japan, there wasn't a man worth me. Great, so runnerup for the stud contest is Tetsurai-san. But I finally clicked on the reason for all the marriage bit: My purpose is to make kids.

Kneeling in dokusan, the smell of incense sitting heavily in the air, made everything seem old and already cured by time, as if it all didn't matter. He was glowing, enraptured in the excitement of his plan for me and my children, he and his "baby," Kannonji. I found myself nodding—everything, anything was okay. Then I caught myself. Wait, hold it, no, that's not what I want. Stop. I thought of my ego, of discriminating consciousness, etc., but still, it's not the life for me. I told Tachibana Sensei that in Japan people don't want to do zazen; in Ireland they do. I wanted to build a dojo over there, I said. Sensei was squirming in his seat; he obviously didn't want to be the one to present Go Roshi with disappointing news and asked why I didn't call everyone over here. That's all I needed, him confounding me when I was so reluctant and so insistent. Go Roshi was laughing, said I was a plane and could fly to Ireland. Tachibana Sensei seemed to be putting things vaguely when I needed to be firm. But it'll all work out in the end, I'm sure; Go Roshi is always changing his mind.

At first I was a bit disappointed not to be going back to Tokyo, but when I came back here it was so overwhelmingly beautiful, the life so pure that I couldn't stay disappointed.

KANNONJI, IWATEKEN
MAY 1981

Dear Mum,

A very happy Mother's day. . . . Are your Japanese plans any more definite? . . . More people are coming to Kannonji now that the weather's improving. Busloads of little old ladies doing the rounds of the temples. A group came yesterday and chanted ancient sutras, ringing bells. Many could no longer carry a tune, but their

cracked voices wavered up and down with touching determination.
Hope you get to see some of them. Do write soon, Ma, and have a
good day. After six of us, you've earned it.

Love ya. M.

May 14

Lately and today specially (I was alone) I've been getting flashes of *tada ["just"]*. Doing something and it's all there is in the entire universe. These arise spontaneously but are so refreshing and different that they attract attention and immediately my discriminating labelling consciousness jumps up to say, "Hey!"

May 15

Tachibana Sensei got really angry with Tetsugen-san. Says he treats me like a thing, a temple attachment, and shows no gratitude. That's an exaggeration, though he treats me often like a maid. I think it's part of the way Japanese men are raised to treat the women in their lives. Now, pretty much I just say "Hai" and do as I'm told. I reckon in the long run it's I who gains and he who loses, I who'll get my ego battered and his that will grow more entrenched. Nevertheless, once he told me to plant *kiku [chrysanthemums]*. (I was already weeding in the rain, right after breakfast, while he sat around digesting.) I quite firmly said I'd go to Sasaki-san's and get them, but I'm not planting them today. He looked shocked and giggled nervously, a bit embarrassed: "Why?" I said I had other work to do. I didn't feel or sound annoyed. Pushing the wheelbarrow down to Sasaki-san's for the kiku, I felt, "Hee, hee, hee, I'm a bitch, I'm terrible, but chuckle, chuckle, I enjoyed that." Then I saw her—skinny, 70, down on the floor vigourously scrubbing the already gleaming wood with such earnestness she didn't even hear my call. I felt ashamed. She trundled into the garden and dug me up kiku from the ends of the rows she'd already neatly trimmed, thinned, and transplanted. She motioned me into the shed, all the time half running, her stooped back parallel to the ground like a cyclist angled for speed. The shed was dark, smelled musty. She took the lids off various barrels, pulling out all manner of salted and preserved vegetables and stuffing them into bags for me. Then "sayonara." She was off about her work. Ashamed, thoroughly ashamed, I bought an ice-cream and pushed my barrow past the rice fields with the radios, the many bent bodies at their jobs. I wondered what they thought about, if they thought at all. Were they all like so many Zen masters, living their koans—digging and digging and only digging?

MAY 18

Yesterday I was in a bad mood. No reason. Felt if there was anyone to interact with even a bit that it would quickly be dispersed. My bad moods usually are. Tetsugen-san came back from the *onsen [hot springs]*, thrust the kettle through the window at me. "It leaks, put it in a bottle" (using the most brusque form of Japanese commands). "When you're done wipe the kettle well or it'll rust." (Again, very curt.) I bristled. Who did he think he was, telling me to fill his bottles in a manner like that? I was about to lash out, but before I could remember the word for slave or servant, he turned on his heels. "Next time, next time," I seethed. I'd had enough of him and his arrogant ways. I'm sick of silently resenting him; it's better for both of us to air it, even if he is my superior. Didn't I feel small, then, to discover later that he'd brought the kettle, filled it, and returned with it, not for himself, but for me.

Today it's pouring rain, but I'm in a great humour. Even yesterday, though, it was totally clear how all these moods just arise and fade, are empty and impotent. Yesterday I felt completely empty. Frighteningly empty. There simply was no me. Not the kind of universal me I sometimes feel— but nothing at all. Void.

Yesterday Ojii-san came on his bike, like a gentle spring breeze that you mightn't notice if you weren't paying attention. He's old and bent with a gait like a fisherman wading out from the sea. He lit incense and bowed to Kannon sama. Then walked very slowly, as if he felt the weight of the sunshine, across to Busshari-To. In his stocking feet he smiled, a golden smile of sweets and dentists and irrepressible good will. He climbed the stairs, doing one thing at a time. Every movement seemed to command his total attention. "No, no tea this time. Next time. Sayonara." Onto his bike. It was green, creaking down the tree-lined alley. The carrier sparkled in the sun. One white butterfly flickered across his path.

Am reading de Beauvoir's biography. Thus far she doesn't appeal to me much as a person. Very arrogant and seems quite cut off from her feelings, or maybe they're just not the public's business, which is fair enough. De Beauvoir and Sartre had no friends and few relationships, she said. I wonder if that kind of isolation is necessary to achieve anything. (I know, I know. There's nothing really to achieve, but until I really realize that, I must go on trying to achieve, though really realizing that there is nothing to achieve.) She spoke of a woman (Camille?) who was writing from 12 p.m. to 6 p.m. every day. It prodded de Beauvoir, and I think, if she's putting in that kind of energy and devotion on something like a novel, how much more I should be putting into my training?

I was thinking about Mariah and how she sent me the cigar two years ago. Was wondering where to get one this birthday when what arrives but a big 40¢ cigar. She's great. I'm still giggling from the card. She also is trying to remember if I'm 27 or 28 (26!); it's a relief to me. Two years ago I felt very old, very afraid of growing old. Now I feel 18; I don't look it, and no one else thinks of me that way, but the world and my relationship to it feels like when I was that tender age.

I'm relishing growing old; as my body decays my spirit is only going to soar all the more.

MAY 19

The morning was rain. Not like yesterday's heavy, pounding rain, but a soft, grey vaporous rain. Went to Sasaki-san for daffodil bulbs. It was cold, we agreed, not like May. Ojiichan loosened them with a big fork. I cleaned them off with a trowel. It took all his strength to lift and aim his blows but each one was perfect. He gave me purple rubber gloves for my bluish hands. He smiled and continued down the row. We filled two boxes with daffodils and narcissi. They were heavy. I washed the rubber gloves in a puddle and gave them back. He was still smiling. I picked my way back in the rain, now more like airborne dew. The mountains were scarcely visible but very present, at once rooted and wispy (like the driving instincts that show themselves as dreams. . .).

Today no post. Pity.

Last night I tried to stay up all night doing zazen. But I dropped off for an hour or two. I was really annoyed with myself because I missed that time of lucidity that comes after the tiredness. Felt very annoyed. However, today all day long "this mind is Buddha" which I read in the *Shobogenzo [writings of Dogen]* struck reverberations in my thoughts. "This mind is Buddha, no mind, no Buddha" suddenly became very clear. They are only echoes of the one.

Strange and charming that in the technologically advanced Japan such anachronisms as the bill collectors exist. No one has a checking account, so they come around on their bikes and scooters collecting. It's much more human. Just now came the waterworks collector on her bike, her little one on her back. He bravely gave me the change. I like him better than the bank tellers.

Circumstances are forever making a fool of me. I should say "teaching me" but I'm a slow learner. Sometimes I bitch about Tetsugen-san and stupid trivial things, the way he jeers when he thinks I'm doing something wrong or silly, how he never closes the door, no longer notices what I cook even when I make his favorite dish. I mused—he has no emotions or heart. It would never occur to him to bring me home a treat, for example; that kind of spontaneity isn't in him. Of course as I thought the thought, he closed the door behind him. Yesterday he brought me home a piece of cheesecake (Yuriko-san had said I like cheesecake), tonight raved about the curry and comfrey tempura I made. Oh, well. I've accepted that once I get to know people they're always good; I always like them (even the Shimoshinge-sans of the world). If only I could actualize Sono's "Thanks very much for everything. I have no complaints whatsoever." Truly each situation is its own perfection. I wish I could uproot the bitch in me that knows, even as it bitches, that it's nonsense and destructive.

I love the cat. (Actually, it just hit me that there's another example. The cat drove me crazy for ages; now she seems the best one I've ever known.)

I've been gathering wild plants and mushrooms. I love strolling with my bucket, seeking them out and bringing them back. Each one has its time of perfection, its tricks in becoming edible. Soak with the bath's ashes, boil three times, grate through the slit in a daikon. . . They have no fertilizers or spray; they're free and it's the same thrill as rescuing the battered chair or leaky pot off someone's rubbish pile. The scavenger, gypsy, make-do renovator in me revels. I was standing by the rice paddies with my pail. The wind was still and the waters unruffled. The sun was streaky through the clouds. Indigos, emeralds merging. Only one violent splash of yellow—huge dandelions reflecting in the water. I was dumbstruck and drawn into it. The cat ran over to me, rubbing my leg, and as I re-emerged it came as a relief to realize that I'm not separate from it. I remember the times I battered the flowers with my pleas to be let inside. Now, for moments, there is no inside and no outside.

I was tired after staying up all night. The tiredness dragged across a couple of days but seemed also to drain my usual discriminating mind. There were many moments of pure absorption. These are still rare, but it's the first indication I've had that my consciousness may actually be changing. I actually enjoy working. The first time that thought flickered across my mind, a voice, almost a reflex, quashed it—afraid someone might hear and take advantage. But Go

Roshi is right. Working *isshoken mei* [with all one's heart and soul] is not work.

MAY 26

The other day Sasaki-san came on her bike. She looked ravishing. She sat on the step where I was scrubbing the floor. A white scarf was draped like the Virgin's veil, draped carelessly on her head. She still has all the mannerisms of a young coquette, darting her eyes playfully, laughing flirtingly into her hands. As she so often does, she brought us some of her good home-cooking. She wanted to play goeka music at the ceremony on the ninth. She prevailed on Tetsugen-san, employing every measure of her female charms. Her eyes were beautiful, pleading and winning. His eyes were on the floor. He often seems to be fascinated by something inanimate when a person's eyes are too intimate, or even real. I wondered if perhaps he was listening with everything he had and if that was why he had to focus on something as undistracting as the concrete floor. She paused, straining for his reply. For a moment he was silent. Then: "Don't wash this floor like in Tokyo or the water will seep underneath and freeze in winter." A short soliloquy about cracked concrete and he lapsed again into silence. She took no heed and continued as if there had never been a gap in the conversation. I could have dumped my bucket on him. How could he be so insensitive to her?

MAY 28

We went to collect plants from one of Sasaki-san's relatives. It was early morning. Misty. The rice fields had not yet been planted and formed spreads of square lakes into the distance, reflecting mountains and clouds, that day a patchwork of blues and greys. We were putting the plantlings into a box. I was handling them rather roughly, thinking more that he was being rather grasping in asking her for more and more, and thinking that I'd have to plant them. My mind was far away from the plants. One tiny one went under the next sod I added. "It's alive, it's alive" she said, not in alarm, not scolding, but as if a self-evident truth were speaking itself while her lips moved. I was ashamed.

My birthday came. Tetsugen forgot. (On his birthday I'd gone to a lot of trouble to make a special cake; he only said it was better to buy one. Sometimes ya can't win.) In the morning I scrubbed windows, smiling that it was my birthday even if the world forgot. But it didn't. I was overwhelmed, tears actually brimming, with the kindness. Tachibana Sensei with four presents and a bottle of German white wine. Chiba-san made me a beautiful *samuè [work outfit]*, loads of underwear, and a strawberry cheesecake. Dominique showered me with presents and good will. She seems to be getting more and more into Zen. Hope she can suspend her intellect a bit.

Life is great. Actually, my body's in bits—a cut that

keeps bursting on my toe, a shin all bruised from falling through a stool while window-washing; during the cold my frostbite re-emerged. Some weird rash or biting is gradually spreading, first my arm and stomach, now legs, neck, and chest. Strange. But the old *atama [head]* is ill. Am working very hard these days, about 12 hours a day without a break. Still the place seems dirty.

MAY 30

A quiet day. A day of wind and weeds and dirty windows.

KANNONJI, IWATEKEN
MAY 1981

Dear Mum,

. . . *I asked Go Roshi if there would be any time when it would be most convenient for your visit. He got very enthusiastic and said "anytime," even if you came in time for next month's big ceremony (when I'll be run off my feet), that would be okay. But* watch out. I'm sure he hopes you'll fall in love with Japan and we'll both stay and live here happily ever after. . . . As for my leaving here, I'm still not sure when. Your point that I should expose myself to Zen as it's adapting itself in the West is, I think, very valid. My problem is two-fold; one, how to break it to Go Roshi and second, whenever I see him actually in front of me I just can't imagine wanting to switch to another Roshi. He is so excellent and now understands me and my level in a way that would take ages to re-establish with someone else. Still, as he's not here right now, I do feel inclined to go back closer to home. Hmmm.

. . . You're right. Things were a bit awkward here with Tetsugen-san, but they've rebalanced. Soon at least one and maybe two from Tokyo should be staying here, which will break up the couple set-up. . . . My plans are still so nebulous that I can't say with any certainty even what continent I'll be on next spring. Anyway, I'm busy these days. Soon Go Roshi, his wife, and two others arrive to stay. Then for the ceremony on June 7th (this temple's 10th anniversary). We're expecting over one hundred people with top Roshis, politicians, reporters, etc. from all over Japan. I always thought I kept this place clean, but I see it now with new eyes and little nooks that haven't been disturbed at all during those ten years. Ah, well, I've nothing else to do but clean, so I'll have it ready in

*time. Am dying to see you. Do practice your Japanese. You'll be
grateful for any little bit you have. . . .*

Love, etc.

June 1

Tetsugen-san made me a *zenpan [chin rest]*. The wood
smells beautiful. The chin is curved; the board is carved. He
inscribed my name and an old Zen exhortation that from
ancient times people have done such hard training and
attained *daigo [great enlightenment]*. It hangs by a royal purple
string. Holding it in my hands, I feel a sort of reverence for
all the hard training that has gone before. However, that
didn't do me much good last night. It's hard to sleep on the
bloody thing.

June 2

I wonder if the Japanese have a higher incidence of
paranoia than Westerners. People are so reluctant to say

something offensive that it helps me understand better why Tetsuro-san was convinced everyone was talking about him behind his back. On the other hand, it's refreshing to be allowed to be naive, to expect the best and see good. Our culture sponsors a cynicism even in its humour.

This morning I read Dogen's commentary on Gensha's one bright pearl. During zazen, I kept repeating, "The entire universe is one bright pearl." I felt luminous. Everything really was a divine light. Couldn't help smiling. If that had been a koan, I'd have to say "There is no pearl, no universe, only BRIGHT."

Dear Mum,

. . . Here things have calmed down a bit after the 10-year anniversary ceremony. So, Mum, are you definitely coming to Japan? Your trip to Ireland in September is right when I was expecting you. Maybe you'd be best getting one of those "round-the-world-with-

stopovers" tickets and come to Japan from Ireland. Otherwise the £99 London/Hong Kong standby deal might be your best bet. Do let me know as soon as you're definite. It's a pity you couldn't have been here for the ceremony. It was quite impressive. There was a woman priest (first other one I've seen) who told marvellous stories about when she and Go Roshi were young and training together. She set off at 20, walking around Japan, chanting "Namu myoho renge kyo" (the practice of another sect) and visiting various Roshis. She ended up trying to visit my Roshi's Roshi (Harada Sogaku Roshi), but was kidnapped and kept locked away by priests of her own sect. She escaped by climbing out a window and went to Harada Roshi's temple, where they all took her for a boy. She went on and on with great adventures and funny anecdotes—a podgy, little woman, full of vigour. . . .

For the days building up to the ceremony, I'd been working literally non-stop, sleeping just a few hours a night. But somehow the rhythm of everyone working together engendered new energy, and I didn't feel at all tired. So even if you decide to marry all the rest of the kids off in one huge ceremony, no problem—I'll cater! Then, after the ceremony, we did the civilized Japanese thing and went to a hot springs to relax. We all spent the night. (Go Roshi paid everything for me.) Had a big feast and numerous soothing dips in the springs. But then I just went poof. Suddenly, when it was time to enjoy myself, all I wanted to do was sleep. They made all of us give a little self-introduction and sing a song. I got a mischievous pleasure from seeing all the dear little Buddhist ladies oohing and aahing and clapping when I was singing "Take her up to Monto."

Tetsugen-san must have overtired himself getting ready for the ceremony. People, like him, with kidney disorders are said to be prone to depression, and the following week or so he went into a depression black enough to make any of Margy's look like amateur theatrics. I was ready to tell Go Roshi that it's him or me but not both of us! However, to my relief, it wasn't a permanent character change (or the real hidden self), and if anything, since then he's been brighter than ever.

Love, M.

P.S. Guess what's for dinner tonight? Whale and chrysanthemums—these were looking stale on the altar. I feel awful about the whale, but he buys it because it's cheap. Aren't you looking forward to Japanese food, Mum?

JUNE 22

A gap. Much has happened. We prepared for the ceremony. Paul-san and Yokogawa-san came. I saved the wine from my birthday to welcome them. Paul extravagantly gave me Japanese and Zen cookbooks that cost a fortune, and he struggling to keep the shirt on his back and rice in his belly. We toasted and tasted with the wine. It sparkled, but the occasion didn't. There was a tangible stiffness between them. Paul later told me they'd had a falling out. She had been in love with him, a fact that seemed to irritate rather than please him.

The next day Go Roshi was coming. I was busy with last minute preparations. It seemed as if I had been doing nothing but cleaning for weeks and still all around me were little dirt traps, black holes. I finished Go Roshi's birthday cake in the midst of the chaos. It took ages, a challenge to my ingenuity. A cake with no cake pans and only a tiny toaster oven. Paul said it sounded like a koan—"Bake me a cake with no oven." I built tin foil pans, held the door open with a Biro, performing culinary gymnastics of twisting, piercing, covering, and exposing the batter. The result looked decidedly unstable, taller than wide or long, three uneven layers each straining to slide in a different direction. Feeling warm towards Jacuda-san, I saved her some mediocre doughnuts from the day before. She embarrassed me thoroughly by distributing a half each of the by-then-hardened rings to the Morioka *zazenkai [gathering]*.

211

Dominique came to dokusan. She seemed excited. Go Roshi gave her muji—intriguing. Then Tachibana Sensei took us out for coffee.

My own dokusan was incredible. We only talked about the koan, nothing personal as we usually do. But Go Roshi was so beautiful, so radiantly beautiful, he really seemed to shine. Our eyes met, and truly there was no separation, but it was I that was drawn into him. He told me that my training in Kannonji was the best possible, just to throw myself minute by minute into each job. When he said it, it seemed obvious, and I wondered how I could have contemplated training elsewhere. I think I promised to stay three years. I'm not really sure, as I was mostly trying to hold back the tears that promptly overflowed when I left the room. I don't know where they came from. I certainly wasn't sad, but neither was I crying from joy. It just seemed to be an expression of the nameless emotion that had overwhelmed me. The following dokusans only dealt with koans. In "Seizan, Alone and Poor," he gave me a very emphatic full marks. In "Joshu examines the hermits," he said I couldn't even imitate Joshu. Either way is okay.

In one of Paul's dokusans, he encouraged him to help me found a dojo in Ireland. I was thrilled. Maybe he's accepted that alternative.

That evening Go Roshi returned to Kannonji with us. The next morning I was waiting in the dokusan line, alone, the sun soft-shining across the tatami. After breakfast, Go Roshi announced that it was his birthday party. We got out my wobbly cake and the warm beer that Paul had given him. He distributed both. We joked warmly about blowing out the candle, but the universe would be in darkness. "Thank you beery much" to Paul. "Thank you cakey much" to me. We were all laughing.

The rest of the time 'til the ceremony was work without respite. But I didn't even want to rest. I had loads of energy and was riding high on the excitement of everyone being there. All had great spirit and helped tirelessly. Jacuda-san oversaw everything and yet saw to the little things, like that everyone got a cup of tea. Oku-san was there, but Jacuda-san seemed much more Go Roshi's wife and Oku-san a dear sister, whose relationship is rooted in the past.

Yoko-san, too, slaved away. Every time I saw her, she was sweeping or scrubbing a floor. When I called her Kannonji's Cinderella, she put her hands on her hips and leaned back, her teeth seeming huge as she laughed and laughed.

Paul, too, worked with every ounce he had, singing boisterously numbers from the musicals back home as he scrubbed Busshari-To's windows. His job, washing windows, had been started by a young Japanese lad the day before. He'd come asking to stay. Tetsugen was out collecting Go Roshi from the station. I said he should ask him when he got back. He volunteered to work. I gratefully accepted the offer. Things got hectic. He, Paul, various workmen all asking questions and in the midst of it all Naifari-san arrives for ookyo and tea with all the time in the world. The lad worked hard. Tetsugen returned and ordered him to clear off. He wouldn't look at him or explain but merely shouted over his shoulder as he strutted away. I insisted on feeding him lunch. He was quiet and soon went out to continue work on the windows. Tetsugen began abusing him again and ordered him off the premises. Paul and I were furious. We were all going to Morioka for dokusan. I said we should at least take him to Morioka, but Tetsugen refused to take him even as far as the bus. We pulled out. Tears of rage were in my eyes. We live by other people's kindness, and yet he couldn't even spare the kindness one gives a mangy dog in one's path. Paul was equally incensed; his eyes flashed black with what looked like hate, although I don't think him capable of that emotion. Then he cursed Tetsugen for his dictatorial ways, also for not eating the lunch I specially prepared for him. When we returned to Kannonji with Tachibana Sensei, the police were moving the lad away. He had sat down in zazen, refusing to move. Wonderful. Just like the priests of old. Then Tetsugen half convinced me that he was unbalanced, but in retrospect, I don't think so. Paul reminded me about the lad that had been driven away during Takuhatsu. We both sighed and shrugged.

So we worked and then worked. Morioka zazenkai women came and took over the kitchen. They kept asking me where things were, but I didn't know.

Paul's birthday was the 6th. He had left behind invitations for friends to come to the ceremony. I wanted to do something for him, but where was the chance? So at 3:30 in the morning I started baking. Only time for one layer. I went out before the dawn to gather herbs for the cake. The grass was wet with dew of last night's rain, the air misty and cool. Gion-chan followed me, jumping through the long grasses. The mountains were shrouded, revealing yet mysterious, in webs of grey sinking to black. In all the business of preparations, it was a time of stillness, of total quiet. Everyone, even Go Roshi, was asleep. It was my own little oasis in time. Then back into the fever and fun of work.

Tetsubun-san arrived from Tokyo by surprise. Before, my Japanese was never good enough to talk with him, but this time we got on famously. He likes to work, to laugh, to drink beer. His heart is very young for his 50 years, younger than Tetsugen-san who prides himself on his youthfulness (prides himself with all the showiness and trappings of one desperately reassuring himself, as he fades through time).

After it was all over, Tetsubun-san and I sat drinking soda in the summer afternoon sunshine. He said he felt no difference in our ages. But when he said it, 1) it was true and 2) it wasn't to emphasize his youth but an attempt to attribute it to my "mirror zen." Incredible man. Also the only Japanese that I'd call really sexy. When he was leaving, after a couple of beers and blushes, he asked me to say "goodbye" the European way—with a kiss. I was delighted to oblige.

That reminds me, Oku-san's face nearly burst when

Paul kissed me "hello." He's still completely natural about such things, but I'm getting self-conscious with the Japanese. When he found his birthday cake and gifts, I was working in the kitchen. He came upon me from behind, whirled me by the apron strings and kissed his thanks. My first reaction was flustered. Imagine! But also I was very conscious of Yokogawa-san, who could have felt hurt.

Go Roshi was also keeping up a hectic pace. Because of my height, he'd asked me to stick up various bits of paper from above. I, of course, wanted to "really do" the thing, but was so self-consciously "really doing" that the tape stuck to my fingers and things crinkled and split. Sweeping the corridor, I met him popping through the window, one leg in and one leg out, kimono hoisted rakishly. We both dissolved into transcultural giggles.

The night before the ceremony itself, we had a small party. As it was also Paul's birthday, he was heavily toasted. They asked him to sing a song. He opted for a belated "Happy Birthday" to Go Roshi. I crowed along. Go Roshi loved it and called for an encore.

That night we had *bansan [evening sutras]*. Go Roshi didn't come, sending instead the message that he had drunk too much *tamago sake [sake with egg]*. I loved him for that. He never gets drunk or even tipsy, so it was marvelous on the eve of this momentous occasion that he could be so unattached to his image as to send the message that he couldn't come because he was drunk! Jacuda-san was well on, waltzing around the kitchen. In fact, they all seemed to be well-oiled; I'd been doing the washing-up, but that didn't last long enough to account for the fact that I was stone cold sober and they all at least flushed.

Paul came into the kitchen. Everyone must have been pouring him birthday drinks. He looked pleased with himself, pleased with life. But then he blurted out, "They're burying you in there; they don't understand; they love you and are taking turns around the table praising you, but they'll bury you. Go Roshi's not saying a word, but he must be thinking to keep you in Kannonji." He was almost moaning.

The sake must have made them sentimental. Those praises used to really upset me. They made me feel as if I was living a lie, because I certainly wasn't all the wonderful things they say. Now it just seems as if they're talking about another person, and I find it amusing. It's just the Japanese way. (One of the things they must have said is that now I look Japanese. Two different people said so lately—it sure is as if they're talking about some other person.)

The ceremony itself went off grand. I rang the bell as they filed in. A few roshis came, but not as many as last year. There was a small, pudgy woman monk. Her face when at rest looked like a surly old man nursing the ulcer he deserved from an overindulgent life. Her bald head and unfeminine features but girlish voice combined to give the impression of an aging eunuch. Then she spoke. She came alive. I couldn't understand all the words but couldn't miss her spirit. She seemed to be popping. Her sentences were punctuated by excited dashes of her fist and comic sweeps through the air.

Her tiny frame seemed to balloon as she'd stretch, illustrating some yarn.

Tetsugan-san also came to the ceremony. Go Roshi thanked him for publishing his books. He was, as always, absolutely radiant. Dom saw it too, a light from him that is almost blinding.

After the ceremony we went to the *onsen [hot springs]*. Then a terrible tiredness flooded over me. I slipped into the hot mineral water with every cell in my body drooping. I was scarcely able for the party, a bit of an anti-climax.

Perhaps Tetsugen-san overstrained himself, too. He went into a black depression that seemed endless. Didn't talk to me except to ridicule me and give orders in the gruffest possible Japanese. The common greetings that mean nothing but symbolize a multitude, he dispensed with. I was biting back the resentments, chastising myself for my intransigent ego. "Good morning"—a deaf ear, still tongue, where's the difference? Tetsubun-san had stayed an extra day to help. Tetsugen-san was the soul of cheer and humour for the moment. They both exuded the fun and laughter of schoolboys on the bounce. Then suddenly into the pits of gloom. He confronted me.

What had I done? I wracked my brain. I tried to be light and normal, which he seemed to find very irritating. I almost respect him for that, for refusing to be seduced by my false entreaties. False they were, as I was choking with hurt, yes, really hurt. That "non-existent" ego was bleeding.

During that time, I spoke with no other living soul. Gion-chan tried very hard to bridge the chasm to humanity. She ran if he so much as picked his nose. Ten long days. Ten days of thinking this was his true personality; this was the future mapped out for the next year and a half. I was ready to tell Go Roshi I'd take care of Kannonji alone, that it's me or him.

Then it broke. As suddenly and completely as it came, it cleared. Last spring (about the time he proposed), he had ordered me a new set of summer robes. They arrived, and with great pleasure he gave them to me. With great relief I received them. His first civil words. I thanked him profusely, but it was less for the robes (which I didn't need) and more for reprieving me.

Sasaki-san phoned. I nipped down on my bike, by the brook and across the rocky roadway. She motioned me into her dark kitchen, the bare wood beams glowing. She was rubbing salt into large fresh sardines (iwashi). That room always seems timeless, as if nothing had changed since long before she was born, but she was bouncing up and down on her hunkers, flapping her hands and telling me her schedule in a hurried voice. Up at 4 o'clock, cleaning, light the rice, clean the altar, go to Kannonji, make everyone's breakfasts and lunch bentos, then o'soji [cleaning]. Yet she always finds time to come to ookyo and to give us her goodness. Suddenly she grew quiet and still. She was no longer speaking from agitation, looked me straight in the eye, unwavering, and says "All I ask is that when people come they say the old lady is kind." My heart wrenched. She knew all the backbiting that Morioka's zazenkai deal her even though she had donated the land and is so devoted.

I love the very same ladies that do it to her, but those pleading eyes. . . . "That's all," she said, "and then I can be happy—now these sardines are secret; the young ones will be annoyed that I'm giving them away." She was sure I understood. I was choked and couldn't think of words. I could only bow deeply, then up and off on me bike.

Chiba-san invited me to a concert where a Japanese woman was playing the harp, Irish style. They said it would go on late. This was all a ruse so that I'd be allowed to stay the night with them. Chiba-san asked Tetsugen-san, who said they were to bring me back after breakfast, but when she asked, he said I should be back by five in the morning. Nonsense. He just didn't want to get up and do service. The concert itself was so-so, but then we went back to their house and ate dinner and drank beer. The rain was falling and the air smelled sweet. He opened a sliding door, lit an oil lamp, and in the flickering darkness we listened to the pattering of the rain. We sat drinking and chatting. It was a bit nostalgic, a thing I always love, just to natter with good friends. Don't often get the chance. The dictionary required squinting in the dark but somehow we managed, in fact til 3:30 in the morning. I'd been up for 24 hours by then but felt incredibly high from their warmth and the occasion. I don't really mind having to do the dishes, but not having to do them, not cooking (though I did that before I left), plus a steaming mug of percolated coffee, all thrilled me. Things I used to take so for granted. There was no way I'd be back before breakfast. Chiba-san, who makes no bones about disliking Tetsugen-san, just told me to take things easy. It was a rainy morning. Coffee and toast for breakfast and fresh tangy yogurt. We looked at pictures, smelled roses, discussed the twittering sparrows and shedding dog. I knew Tetsugen was probably getting more and more annoyed, but I didn't give a tinker's damn. Whether it was from tiredness or from joy, I don't know, but that whole morning I was in some kind of blissful samadhi. "Moment after moment." If that's what it's all about, then it's worth it. Nothing could bother. Everything, from the rain-glistening mountains to the dog's filthy pawprints on my clean kimono, was wonderful. It grew later and later. Chiba-san still didn't ring. Ah, well, might as well be hung for a sheep as a lamb, I thought, as we headed, not homewards, but to the tamago farm.

They had been telling me about it for a long time, but still I was unprepared for how it would take me. They had brought me to my place, to my life. It was drizzle-pouring. Black hens bespeckled the place like some insistent mildew. Everything I looked at was dotted with them, and each dot would be not one but a cluster, on steps, stools, stones, an abandoned wreck, a tumbly shed, haystacks, anything stationary—strutting, calling, laying, and reminding me of my childhood. They guided me into the large dark old farmhouse.

The first room had a mostly dirt floor with one raised

section of black wood beams. It smelled of the good damp earth. In the centre was a huge tree trunk turned into a table, and every surface was covered with bouquets of fresh or dried flowers. The man of the house spoke deep into my insides. What was it? Maybe it was the way his eyes never wavered, so that I was barely aware of what he said but only absorbed in the depth of him. [The sitting room was also dark, the darkness of soot and wood. A huge square open hearth had no chimney, so the smoke curled up, up towards the ceiling, but wearying on the journey, sifted downwards. Our eyes stung pleasantly. Then he carried in a huge pile of kindling bound with straw and fed the fire. His smile came straight from his *hara*. The woman twinkled, dimpled, wiping her hands on her apron, smoothing it across her sparse hips. She made *mat-cha [tea]* for us, a long ritual of wiping and whirling the universe into a bowl. She knelt by the fire, dipping water from the soot-encrusted cauldron. Slowly, almost caressing her utensils, she poured. Her features were dim in the soft light of the room, but one side glowed colours thrown up by the fire. I was drawn into her every movement.

I knew we should be getting back. Tetsugen would probably freak, but truly time was hardly conceivable. Could there really be a future or a past or anything besides this room, this woman with her frothy tea?

It was the anniversary of his mother's death. We did ookyo before a little altar reeking of incense. Chiba-san finally decided we must leave. Pity. The woman was busy making mochi. I wanted to stay, wanted to work hard for them.

The scenery coming home was spectacular. It was still rainy. Tetsugen was still in bed. He wasn't too angry. We were so very late, it was such a complete affront that he was already beaten. "*Dameda [no good]*," he said.

They put me on the radio. The interview was in Japanese, and I didn't understand one of the questions. There was a very long (for radio) pause, awkward (for the interviewer) silence. Well, that's a difficult question, she said. I wonder what it was. I had to laugh.

Tetsugen went into another depression. First he was just nasty for a few days. He scarcely spoke, and then it was always curt and mean. I was getting fed-up, but was trying to tell myself that it was only my ego. Then one time—again it was trivial, and I was revolted by my pettiness—he was snapping orders. I always obeyed, but under my breath, murmuring "I hate you; I hate you." That shocked me. Listen, Mors, you've never hated anyone in your life. You know full well he's decent. It's not him you hate, but the way he treats you. Whatever it is, this isn't healthy. So I blurted it out to him, gently, apologizing, saying, "I just don't like the way you treat me. I'm human, too, not your servant or a dog." That doesn't sound gentle in retrospect, but at the time it seemed inoffensive, perhaps only compared to what I was feeling. He laughed, in embarrassment, I think. By the time I'd finished banka, he'd gone to bed.

For three days he stayed locked in his room. At first I thought maybe he was dead. I felt shockingly unperturbed. Several times I called to him. He answered that he was okay, but he didn't come out. Was he trying to punish me in some way or just so sick of everything that he wouldn't come out? It was peaceful. When he finally appeared, he was surly, his skin a sickly grey, stubbled. For the next 48 hours, he only snarled at me to wash my filthy feet and get him the Sensei's money. But something had snapped in me. I didn't care about him anymore, so I was free of him. He could say what he liked to me, hate me if he liked. It didn't matter so the whole thing became rather amusing. I felt a bit of a cruel bitch to be laughing at his misery, but it was a lot better than going under with him.

Then he came up from it.

Go Roshi came for zenkai. Dom came to consult with Go Roshi and asked a million questions, wanting everything to be rationally amenable. It wasn't.

After zenkai, coming home, the light was on in the kitchen. Strange. A bald head. It was Shimo-san. I couldn't believe it. It was late and I was tired, but I managed to throw something together for him to eat. The next day, early, Tetsugen phoned Go Roshi, who said to throw him out. Easier said than done. He had no money, he said. Tetsugen brought him to the station, but Shimo was back at Kannonji before him. There's something in him I admire. He's a very free man. Doesn't give a damn about much of anyone or anything. But his being there made allies of Tetsugen and me, us against him as it were. We sat on the roof chopping stray branches and laughed about mad Shimo-san. They say it's Zen sickness, that he used to be normal but overdid his Zen training and went a bit bonky. He was marvelous, though. Here we were busily throwing him out, and he had guts enough to do banka. I do enjoy that kind of guts. I stopped feeding him, and he left peacefully enough, first ascertaining exactly when sesshin would be.

It struck me that cats can do no right or wrong. Is that because they have no ego, or because right and wrong are our mental constructions? Even when Gion kills, it is not wrong.

JULY 11

Several mornings of samadhi. For the first time I woke up, still actually sitting. Got the news that Galli-san was coming early to prepare for sesshin. He came and we had fun. Tetsugen went to hospital and left Galli a pile of wood and an electric saw. We climbed a tree, listened to the wind blow and the rice grow. For lunch I made an improvised spaghetti with *soba [buckwheat noodles]*. We sat on the veranda of the founder of the Soto sect's room, looked across the rice paddy, and toasted each other with lunchtime saké and ice cream. Then he went back to work and I pulled weeds. I heard him shrieking, "Mora-san! Mora-san, my finger!" At first I thought he was joking, but the saw was still running, and his voice sounded hysterical. His hand was gushing blood. I put on a makeshift bandage and we ran to the road, his hand up in the air. I stopped a car and got him into the hospital. Everyone was staring. We must have looked a sight, both filthy and ragged, his T-shirt spattered with blood and me in my wellies. It was a very nasty cut, right through the bone. They patched him up. He still worked hard, helping me prepare for sesshin.

Yokogawa-san came. She was preoccupied, worried about how her dog would settle in. She slept in the shed with the dog so he wouldn't be upset. I had promised to help Mia-chan, a semi-paralyzed girl; the kitchen was understaffed; I had the official priestly serving duties, and I badly wanted to do dokusan. But so often I'd be nearly at the head of the line when I'd have a job to do. I got in about three times in all. At night I stayed up doing zazen, scarcely sleeping, and any free time seemed to be absorbed. Tessai-san wanted his clothes mended. Dom or Mia-chan needed a shoulder to cry on.

Dom fizzled out. She had some incredibly strong resistance in her. She had to phone her mother in London and talk for 45 minutes. Several times she ran away, became very vehement. Mia-chan, on the other hand, at first didn't seem to be putting herself into it, but by the end had gotten a lot out of it.

I was tired and still pushing myself. It was great having Galli-san as an ally. In the zendo he'd be doing *jonin [meal-server]*, walking slowly with dignity (and a plastered fist) round the hall, holding the kyosoku, me carrying the buppan. We'd catch one another's eyes and suppress smiles. At those times, it felt as if we were everyone's parents, taking care of them, helping them on this great thing. He said, "I can't be serious with you around." It was mutual. He went to dokusan, and Go Roshi said he should marry someone doing training, like Yokogawa-san. Galli-san said no, that he wanted to marry me. He told me, warning me that Go Roshi might mention it.

I was waiting in the dokusan line, frustrated because Tekkan-san wouldn't let Mia-chan cut in and she could never make it to dokusan. Galli-san was at the front of the line. Tetsugen-san wasn't there, so Galli told me to take his own place. I asked him to give it to Mia-chan. Chiba-san struggled up the stair slowly, like some dogged animal, with her on his back. Galli-san was helping. They bowed. That bow was so beautiful that tears involuntarily streamed down my face for 10 minutes. I listened to the mu's, felt their pain and their hope, a pain and hope of my own, a nostalgia and joy. Again I wept.

In this overly sensitized state, I went to dokusan. Go Roshi told me I was to marry Tetsugen-san on September 18th and stay in this temple. I said I didn't want to. He was pushing me, pushing hard. It was killing me to refuse him. I loved him so very, very much, and he was being so insistent, thinking of everything to induce me. I begged him not to ask, no, not that. Finally I broke down and told him something of Tetsugen's two characters and of my dreams for Ireland. He said he'd think it over. I went out in tears, became quite hysterical. Tachibana Sensei was upset and so was Galli-san. They took me outside. I knew I was being ridiculous.

All along I realized my reaction was all out of proportion to the situation. We were walking back towards the zendo when my legs gave way. I fainted. Galli-san laid me down in the entrance to Busshari-To and shouted to Jakudasan. I only wanted a cup of tea. They brought me inside. Everyone was fussing. I couldn't understand—just a cup of tea. I tried to calm them, tried to stand up, but collapsed twice. They were worried, massaging my feet, applying carbon, and discussing cures.

Something left me, some huge oppressive weight that I'd never even known was there and only recognized in its lifting. I felt so light. I was laughing and crying. Euphoria. They were alarmed. I assured them I'd never felt so wonderful in all my life. (Tetsugen-san had nothing to do with it any more; he was merely the trigger.) My breathing was a kind of panting, as if mounting to some emotional climax. Galli told me to breathe deeply, to do zazen. I tried. My breathing stopped. My mind never felt so clear or lucid. The voices were very far away. I was in a crystal paradise. Galli was screaming at me to breathe. From somewhere I heard my voice softly answering, "Hai." In the distance Tetsugen was calling the hospital. What an effort. But I'd have to show them I was okay. I snapped out of it, sat up, normal as hell. "You see, I kept telling you I was okay." They were relieved, but I only wanted to do zazen. I stayed up doing zazen, but I was too tired for it to be much good.

Next day, Go Roshi said "Until last night you were human trying to become God; now you're God. I'm Buddha." He shook my hand. "We must help the others."

He said it would be all right for me to go back to Ireland after three years.

I was looking forward to living with Yokogawa-san. She has a very quiet, strong, and beautiful nature. When she smiles, it's like the August sun in February, and even my toes have to smile back. At the end of sesshin, during the big party, I was pouring her some beer. She began to cry, threw her arms around me and said she was crying from happiness. I was confused. She didn't seem happy—maybe it was all the build-up and not getting kensho. I was very moved, though, to see her, a Japanese woman, openly displaying such a depth of emotion (though everyone else seemed to find it ridiculous). The next day she left to bring her dog home and never came back. Tetsurin-san (with whom she was apparently having an affair) phoned several times and said it was decided at shosan that I'd return to Tokyo and she'd stay at Kannonji.

For the first time, I really believed I'd return there, and I put my luggage in order, started to bid my good-byes. Tetsugen was freaking, asked me to refuse. I said that if Go Roshi told me to go to Toshoji, I'd go there; if he said Kannonji I'd stay there. He said he needed me. I was his Kannon sama. He mourned the garden that would fall into ruin, his health that would collapse. I was aloof to his protest and felt that life with just the two of us there was sucking at me like the whirling vortex of a drain dragging me down, to swallow and drown me. To have had three of us there, almost any three, to break the couple structure, would have been a relief.

But of course all this was only imaginings of my own construction. Yokogawa-san didn't come back and Tetsurin-san ran away from Toshoji, so I mentally sketch in a romantic elopement and feel happy for them—but stranded myself with a rising tide.

Sasaki-san was also very put out when we thought I might be transferred. It was understandable, what with all the bitching and back-biting that goes on, that it would be natural for her to want an ally here. As a result, when the politicking for a successor at Kannonji arose, Sasaki-san agreed to accept Tetsugen under the condition that for as long as I remain in Japan I'd be kept at Kannonji! And Go Roshi gave his consent.

Strange. . . . Yokogawa-san didn't even stay one day beyond sesshin, yet her presence brought me closer to leaving Kannonji and left me further from leaving than ever before. I had a sinking feeling, a trapped feeling. Tetsugen couldn't suppress a slightly smug smile. I refused to admit I was a bit disappointed, to acknowledge that in his pathetic way he'd won. But then, the stirring thing—whether the thought of losing me, the security of being given Kannonji, or whether something happened in sesshin, I have no idea, but he was a changed man. Still occasionally bossing me, but also actually treating me with respect. We became two equals cooperating in a partnership. His whole disposition is sunnier. I keep waiting for it to pass, for the depression to set in, but it doesn't seem imminent.

After sesshin came the massive job of cleaning up, of hauling out all the futons and covers, pillows to be aired (twice), washing all the sheets, *oryoki wrappers [eating bowl covers]*, futon covers in the tiny, not automatic washing machine. It took days, and before it was really finished I had to start cleaning in preparation for Go Roshi's return and *obon [summer remembrance festival]*.

Shimo-san arrived again. I have to laugh and admire his bull-dog tenacity and thick skin. Roshi permitted him to stay for obon and help us as rusu-ban with Abe-san. In Toyko everything had gone mad with everyone either being asked to leave or running away. No more priests.

I was busy. Some mornings we left as early as 5 or 6. I'd have to get up the buppan, fix the day's food for Abe-san and Shimo-san, offer ookyo, come back, start cooking, light the bath fire, do washing and mending, soji, etc., etc. I did the soji in Go Roshi's room as I waited in dokusan line. It was hectic but okay.

Roshi asked me how many hours I slept. He said that since the war there was no one my equal. I was Irish, he Japanese, but since the war I'm the only one who is his equal. Of course, I'm not. Not at all. But in a sense it gave me something to live up to. Since obon, my practice has improved. We eat earlier, so I have more time for zazen, each day four to five hours, once a week all night. (Well, last night I did doze a couple of hours.) I ram a desk up in front of me, so I really do sleep sitting up and have stopped eating in the afternoon. I'm sleeping about five to five-and-a-half hours a night. Some days I feel as if I'm near some kind of awakening, because my consciousness is different, spontaneously, truly losing itself in menial tasks. Other days, more cynical days, like today, I think I'm closer to a "sleepening." That's only because I'm tired and too half awake for my mind to make the effort to run around; it's all I can do to guide my hand peeling the potatoes.

Of late I feel ridiculously happy. No reason. Just bursting with joy. I remember when I was young, deciding to commit suicide at 26. Once one hit 30 one was over the hill, so 26 was far enough to live. I reckoned that if I hadn't got done by then whatever there was to be done, I never would, so I might as well end it. Now I'm 26, and I feel as if I've lived my life. Strange sensation. Almost as if I'm close to death. Any desires, ambitions, hopes I may have had have either been fulfilled or spontaneously dissipated. I'm totally content. Of course, I want to get deeper, see clearer, but even if I could only have this paltry, shallow awakening, I'd be quite satisfied. Facing into a long, cold winter is not only fine, but I know I'll enjoy it. Everything seems wonderful. Even undesirable, painful conditions have a poignant beauty and exaltation. So in a sense I feel I have died; for myself there is nothing else to strive after, nothing more to make my life worthwhile or to justify it. At 26, a living corpse and such a life!

I'd be embarrassed to tell anyone, it sounds so wishy-washy, but now I have maybe 50 or 60 years (who knows?) of time, of a life, open, blank, ready to offer. I want to live it for other people. What else is there to do with it? Not that I expect to change the world or even a blade of grass, but it's as if to give myself is all I can do, as the flowers have no choice but to blossom. At the moment the best I can see to do is to give to people this freedom, this bliss, and how better than through zazen? So I must go deeper and deeper and work hard, no longer for me but for everyone I can help. And still I can't save anyone. They must work themselves, and not every one will. Thus I should also work politically, work to make people's surroundings that much more tolerable, work for a society that fosters more spiritual, more human, values. A society for people, not profits. What better way to instill the Bodhisattvic spirit in people? But they should work for each other, not for personal gain, and they shouldn't have to worry about economic muck.

Who knows but God-as-a-person may be tentative. We as people don't exist, nothing exists, yet for ease in conversation and life in general we use names and ascribe a tentative existence to ourselves and things around us. In such a way, perhaps, a personal God could be said to exist, but only in this labelling, not fundamental, degree, but existentially.

In a sense, though not his sense, Descartes was right—I think, therefore I am. It is the reflexive thinking that creates the isolated subject.

PART VIII

Mom's Visit

Dear Mum,

Great to hear from you and to know that you are still coming. Things have become a little complicated at this end, but being adaptable as you are, things should work themselves out.

Poor Go Roshi is really near the brink of death. He has lost a tremendous amount of weight from stomach cancer. His doctor says he's already a unique case in the medical history of Japan, to have lived this long. It's pure will power, but at the last sesshin he collapsed and said it might well be the last one he could give. But he doesn't stop pushing himself, keeping up a teaching and ceremonial schedule that would defy two young, healthy men to keep up between them. He told me that he's only extending his life to wrap up unfinished business. That's why I feel really infuriated at the ingratitude of the Toshoji priests who ran away. However, sorry, I got into a diversion. What I meant to explain is that there's no one to send up here. (He may get new monks but they would be very raw recruits.) So I won't be very free for touring. However, suppose I came down to Tokyo to meet you and we spend a couple of days doing Tokyo? (We could stay in Toshoji if you can stand the schedule.) Then we could come to Iwate. There are many day trips and local excursions we could make from here. . . . I'm wondering if you'll still be here October 1st to 5th. I had signed up for sesshin then (thinking your visit would be in September). Aside from the fact that with no priests I'll be needed, I also really want to do this one. I was so busy in the kitchen at the last one that I scarcely got to dokusan and, as I said, this may well be the last one. If you were still here at that time you could do it, too. It would be a unique "inside glimpse" for you. About a third to a half are first-timers, and it would also probably be very good for you. . . . I won't be coming back with you. I'd like to do one more takuhatsu (begging) before I go back, though if Go Roshi doesn't last that long, I might just return before then. At the moment we're right at the edge of a typhoon. Also, it would be a good idea to have a small stash of gifts for the people who will inevitably overwhelm you with kindness. How's your Japanese? During sesshin the TV people came out and did a stint, including me doing dokusan and a small interview. Not only did I have to make a fool of myself with my wretched Japanese, but they also had me translating for Galli-san. Wisely they added subtitles for his bit.

See you soon, M.

Dear Mum,

. . Remember my casually mentioning that we were at the edge of a typhoon? Well, it hit. The worst one in 33 years. (They seldom come this far north.) I was enjoying the warm winds and feeling of excitement. We had to do a special sutra-chanting for about 60 people in Morioka, so we went into town. (I did Ino [invocation reader] *for the first time before such numbers.) On the way back, we were quite amused by the flying chimneys, downed signposts, and overturned bus shelters. It wasn't quite so amusing when we got back to Kannonji and in the pouring rain with pathetic hand saws had to saw our path in. Loads and loads of trees are down, my poor little garden quite leveled, branches and dirt every-where and all inside the building, too. What a sight! Me, enjoying the winds so much, had left my window wide open. It was so full of tree bits and leaves that you'd have trouble recognizing it as a room at all except for the soggy remnants of human habitation. We'll be ages cleaning up after it. Anyway, it's over and it was exciting. . . .*

Hurry over, etc, M.

Dear Nana,

. . . Mum left the day before yesterday and now I'm back in Kannonji. . . . She will fill you in on all the details of what we did. I freeloaded on all her entertainment and did more feasting and sightseeing in that time than I've probably done all told. Poor Mum started with a dose of culture shock but bounded back admirably so that even the Japanese were commenting on her adaptability. . . . Mum's last week was a wild whirl as we had a retreat in Tokyo. The kitchen was understaffed, but Mum jumped right in. She was a born turnip beveller, mushroom fanner, and even without a knowledge of Japanese, she would nip off on the bike (terrorizing the neighborhood) and pick me up the last minute bits as the meal approached count-down. I'm sure she'll have plenty of tales with which to regale you.

Love, Maura

Dear Mama-san Rootu,

When I got back the place was in a right mess. The "gnome" [Tetsugen] hadn't done any housework and had left up the same offerings, so even the tea was turning mouldy. A lot of the leaves are turning, and they're taking in the rice. Wish you could see it. The mornings, however, have been dipping down below freezing. I got my salvia and a few other things up and drying, the begonias inside, widened all the flower beds at the front of the house, put down a ton of bulbs, and now I'm trying to clean up the typhoon damage, so I'm out chopping wood every day. I got the log border made at the back. (Me and the wheelbarrow—very long logs. It was hilarious.) But it looks great, as if it always belonged there. We're going to try a sand garden in the square between zendo and hondo. So I'll make my mistakes here and do a perfect job at home. Tachibana Sensei (who sends his best) and I have started translating Go Roshi's book, so I seldom get to bed before 10:30 and he, poor man, a good 45 minutes later. It's very slow going, but my Japanese and his English are improving. I've started teaching English at the Yoshida's (remember the

241

concert people?) It's great getting out once a week, and she's been teaching me a lot about traditional temple cookery. I never knew her that well before, but I find her stimulating, in fact, inspiring, company—extremely enjoyable and civilized evenings. . . .

Yomiuri Shinbun, one of the three major national newspapers, did a half page special interview with me. Actually I said almost nothing. The gnome prattled away, full of exaggerated praise. Now the TV people are pushing me to do an interview on a morning talk show, but I really don't want to. I'm sick of all this publicity nonsense—though there are some advantages. When I came back from Tokyo, I got a terrible craving for ramen [Chinese noodles] *and searched all over the station for a ramen shop. Anyway, on the bus home, a neighborhood fellow who'd read about me in the local magazine came over to me. He owned a ramen shop and insisted on bringing me for a meal and then driving me home. It really quite took me aback.*

I've started my novel, though I really don't know if I should. Remember at first I was stuck for themes? Now I find there are loads of things I really want to say, and the characters are taking on a life of their own. It's really strange. One feels almost like a medium, as some of them, based originally on people I know, are just spontaneously insisting on their own personalities. Even the heroine, who was originally based on me, now, although she has many of my experiences, has quite different reactions to them. It astounds me, for I wonder where they are coming from. Funny feeling. So all around

242

the temple I have odd pages where I jot down notes as they occur to me. I've also started to write the thing itself, and this is why I say I don't know if I should. But now that there are things that I care about saying, and communicating properly, I find it disturbing that my English has turned so strange. As I read what I write, it has an awkwardness that is coming from having Japanese sentence patterns foremost in my mind. This seems inevitable as long as I'm here.

As for the poor old suitor [a priest heading a temple in Sendai], when I came back here from sesshin, I decided I'd had quite enough of this mooning business. So I wrote him an express letter making it quite clear that I wouldn't marry him. I didn't go so far as to point out the irreconcilable differences—like that I could never keep up with his laundry. But I was to-the-point, and the poor thing got such a shock that mysteriously the muscles of his Achilles tendon or something seized up, and he's been hospitalized for a month. He blames it entirely on his "great disappointment" but I'm relieved that he'll have a month to get over his "great disappointment" before I have to face him again. Anyway, m'dear, I've prattled on long enough, and I want to clean the hen house before the rain that's gathering . . . P.S. It seems you, too, may be in Go Roshi's next book. In one of his lectures he was criticizing the Japanese for only being religious for ceremonies and at their convenience, and he praised you for being determined to go to mass even when away from home, without the language, and at the risk of getting lost. . . .

Love, M.

Dear Mum,

Things certainly sound hectic at your end, and I imagine will stay busy right through Christmas. My book is slow, only about 4000 words to date, but really the hardest part is beginning. I still can't decide on whether to use the first or third person. I feel whichever one I choose will make it a different book. So far, I keep switching—1st person seems more vivid, but I actually enjoy writing more in the 3rd person. Strange. . . . I feel the lack of literature in my own background. While I always read, I preferred nonfiction as being somehow closer to "truth," "reality," etc. Of late I feel tremendously excited. I always thought that writing analytical books about Zen seemed so un-Zen. It set up structures, distinctions, and invited argument and speculation. The novel, on the other hand, requires the sympathetic understanding of the reader. If it's successful, he'll leave his own ego and "become" the character suggested, at least for the length of reading. This is much closer to a Zen understanding (intuition, even?). Really, Mum, I've seriously been considering studying English. That must seem funny to you.

T.C.D. [Trinity College, Dublin] sent me the standard boring forms about post-grad. At least in Sociology and Oriental Religions there's a deadline for applications. These are also formal courses, a fact which has its advantages and disadvantages. I really can't decide anything without talking to the professors involved and being clearer myself about which is the discipline through which I can best express my nondisciplinary ideas. . . . We got a nasty cold snap, snow and the lot. Even the old-timers were surprised, and some of them were caught without the rice in. I'm frantically chopping wood. Tetsugen-san is very thoughtful about standing looking over my shoulder and pointing out what I'm doing wrong. Still, his heart's in the right place, and he shocked the life out of me yesterday by helping me sweep. . . .

Love, M.

KANNONJI, IWATEKEN
DECEMBER 5

Dear Mum,

. . . Try to do a bit of zazen every day, even if its just ten minutes. You really sound great. When I first came to Toshoji and the researchers tested me (remember?), they were surprised I'd only been at it for three months and thought I had surely meant to say three years. They concluded that I had a "natural" talent for it. I'd say you do, too. . . . You asked about Go Roshi's health. Not good. At the end of October they found 5 new lumps. They don't know

whether they're benign or malignant but want to open him up immediately. He says he's too busy. (He just had a sesshin in Kyushu; now it's one in Toshoji and New Year's is the busiest time for a temple.) So he won't go in until January. . . . This translation stuff is very slow. My own book is also slow, but I have an appointed time each day, and whether the muse flows or not, I write. . . .I've found a classical station on Ok'san's radio. This morning I was making pickles, watching the snow fall and listening to (believe it or not) the Boston Pops—heaven in my own dingy kitchen. . . .

Love, M.

KANNONJI, IWATEKEN
DECEMBER

Dear Mum,

. . . Thanks for the books. I'm half-way through Zen and the Art of Motorcycle Maintenance. Rather than making me all Zen-ized, I'd love to get a motorcycle—or at least have access to one to repair it. The other books look as if they'll tide me across many a pub-less evening.

I really missed you and Paul during sesshin. Even that

strange old lady last October was another pair of hands. This time it
was just me and Kondo-san, with larger numbers. Still it went off
okay. One or two fiascos, like when I was using the carbon lamp to
treat Go Roshi before dinner, but I didn't have the time to stay
there, so he asked me to arrange newspapers to avoid a draught.
Since it was chilly, I put on loads of them. Then the whole load
went up in flames. Got the fire out, cleaned up the mess, but with
only 5 minutes 'til dinner, I still had no soup made or meals on
plates. What an exercise in concentration in the midst of chaos! But
we made it in time. Afterwards I just lay down on the floor with a
sack of rice as a pillow and fell asleep. Kondo-san (remember?
always fixing you sandwiches) was marvellous, like an extension of
my own arm, often anticipating what I needed done and totally
responsible. A blessing.

The Deguchis came up from Nara for the occasion and send
their best. Tetsumon-san and the little lady who gave you the fan
send greetings, too.

Thanks to Tetsumon-san, who always sent me up to the top
of the dokusan line, I got my share. Dokusan was also very stimu-
lating, perhaps the best yet. I've gone on to a more difficult book of
koans (and skipped one). Go Roshi is being quite severe about the
koans but explains "A Roshi is like your mother, who comes half
way round the world to make sure her grownup daughter is all right,

so no matter how good a student is, a Roshi will worry and push and push." (Although he always tells me in dokusan that I'm useless, apparently in one of his lectures he said that I'm the only successor to the Zen heart in Japan today!) He exaggerates, but it's nice. . . . A little old lady just came for a ceremony. Then another one came bringing me pickles. She's been out of sorts lately, and the bicycle trip with the pickles seems to have been too much for her. I told her to lie down for a while, and she's gone sound asleep.

When changing for the ceremony just now, I put on the leg warmers you sent. They're brilliant, make a world of difference. (My pickles lady just popped her head up and down. Life in Kannonji is as thrilling as ever.)

The greatest blessing you sent will be that can opener. During the sesshin I cursed a string of curses such as would put all Japanese tin openers out of action eternally. Right at a very busy time I had eventually to bash my tin open. . . .

I'd love to be with you at Christmas. In the supermarket in Tokyo they were playing "Jingle Bells," but there was no holly or tinsel or turkey or Christmas spirit. I know that dear Tachibana Sensei will play Santa Claus, but it's not the same. I suppose it won't do any good my brooding over it; still, I love Christmas. New Year will never take its place. Have fun and a good big feast and a peaceful family Christmas.

Love, M.

KANNONJI, IWATEKEN
DECEMBER 30, 1981

. . . We're in the middle of a funeral. The procedures last for days. All morning yesterday was the bedside sutra, then at night 'til very late the mourners gathered in his home and more sutras. Today is the cremation—more sutras and tomorrow the funeral proper. The funeral and a big meal (I only found out last night!) are to be held here, so I'm up to my eyes in cleaning, sutras, New Year preparations, a mountain (no exaggeration) of beans that must be shelled, and I have to teach tonight. Never a dull moment. . . . Hope you all had a brilliant Christmas.

Love, M.

KANNONJI, IWATEKEN
DECEMBER 1981

Dear Nana,

. . . Mum may have told you that I'm teaching English to a temple family that she met. While, to be honest, I wasn't crazy about the idea at first, but it has worked out wonderfully. The girls, three of them, are extremely intelligent and cooperative, a pleasure to teach (though the differences in levels is a challenge). It's not only an enjoyable evening with an exquisite dinner and a taxi home, but they have adopted us. They have an extremely wealthy temple and enjoy being bountiful; we're by far the poorest in the area. Since I started teaching, though, we haven't had to buy food. She loads me down with goodies that she searches out as not being sprayed, shot, or artificially anythinged (rare in Japan). She's really almost embarrassing. She heard I had a cold, so came all the way out on a snowy day, laden with presents, and she gave up her afternoon to wrap me in steaming ginger plasters. She knows all about old oriental medicine and has been teaching me that, along with cooking. (The ginger plasters really did seem to help.) Now she's trying to arrange that I study flower arranging with her teacher. He's an elderly master trained in Kyoto. She speaks very highly of him, and if her own arrangements are anything to go by, he really is a good teacher. It would be fun to learn. . . . I think of you often with very much love.

M.

PART IX

Completion
1982

Rescued this notebook from a fire. Tessai-san said I should keep a diary. I felt there wasn't time to write feelings and analyze reactions. He said feelings were *moso [something that can distract]*. I said they were not and he agreed, but said a busy person should just write events. Events will recall feelings. This seemed a fitting notebook to use.

The day I found it was in January. I got up at 3 o'clock, shovelled snow, did zazen, woke the others, made breakfast, cleaned up, went out to beg. We had lunch at Okawa-san's (tempura . . . she is kind, remembered that I love it). I came home, gave *Ojisan [uncle]* lunch, cleaned temple, lit fire for bath, made dinner, cleaned up, sorted *momi [chaff]* from rice, talked with Tessai-san (admire him profoundly), did zazen, and went to bed. Takuhatsu was a busy time.

Dear Mum, Scott, and Beth,

Phew! Finally I have a moment to slow down, catch my breath, and write home. I'd been going at the same pace as sesshin for a whole month. Tessai-san came up from Nagano to beg and then stayed 'til the 31st. We walked [begged] every day, and then I finished it after he left. Tetsugen-san walked on the days he wasn't being drained [dialysis], and I hustled people who helped when they could. Two gaijin came from Toshoji and walked four days. Tachibana Sensei, after much initial reluctance ("but Mora-san, I'm over 50"), led us during the winter school vacation and every day he was free from school. He looked so comical squeezed into my robes, his spectacles and grin under the huge straw hat and a polo neck sticking out from under the layers of kimonos. Whenever we needed a smile, we'd only have to shout "Sensei! Student, student," and he'd duck, squirming, pulling the hat down over his face. "No, no, where?"

Mum, you remember Megumi-san, my temple English student? After we'd been walking a few days, I was bemoaning our lack of numbers. She looked up instantly and said, "Well, maybe I'll help." She's a marvel. The next day she was out on the streets looking more of a veteran than any of us, never seemed affected by the cold or the wind, just smiling and chanting. At the end I asked her if she'd do it again next year. This time there was no hesitation. She positively roared "of course." We're the only women who have ever walked in this area, and I suspect she's the youngest to have walked.

Tetsugen's case was close to miraculous. The first couple of days he was wrecked, but after that the walking did him good. Tessai-san also had a positive influence on him. He was shocked that I was literally doing everything while Tetsugen hovered over a stove crying "invalid." Tessai-san wouldn't put up with any self-coddling, and night after night he lectured him. Tetsugen was inspired on the days he was due for dialysis. He'd walk an hour to the hospital, even in storms before paths had been beaten in the snow. I was dumbfounded.

Last year the challenge had gone out of takuhatsu for me, so this year I decided to push myself further. We're allowed to wear socks with the straw sandals, so we usually wear several pairs plus plastic bags to keep out the wet. In the old days, though, the monks used just to go barefoot with the sandals through the snow. I wasn't sure if I could. When the snow melts and refreezes it's just like walking barefoot on crushed ice, but as Go Roshi says, if you just take one step at a time, you can do anything. And it's true. It was fine. The others, except Tessai-san, tried to discourage me; they said it would be too much. He only said if he wasn't so old he'd like to try it too. Then one night we were sitting up late by the woodstove, *drinking tea, with him telling me stories about Go Roshi when he was young. It was then a week before the end of takuhatsu and Tessai-san said, "You see, your limits are mostly in your mind." Then he gulped, as if only realizing for the first time what his words really meant. Then he said, "I've only a week to go, but I'll do it barefoot," and he did.*

So we all learned something and maybe got a little stronger. It was also a lot of fun, maybe the most enjoyable takuhatsu yet; all the walkers got on very well, and it was just plain good fun. Many people gave us meals; Megumi-san's parents did so four times. It was a help, especially for me. I'd be up most days at 3. Then if there was snow-shovelling to do, I'd get it done before zazen time, then sit at zazen, make breakfast, put the offerings in front of the statues, go out and walk, start lunch as soon as I'd walk in the door, get it all cleaned up, and start cleaning the temple, bring in the wood (give the chickens their hot water bottle), light the fire for the bath, take down the offerings, make dinner, clean up, wash the rice, prepare the next day's vegetables, do laundry, shell beans, take a lukewarm bath, and conk out for a few hours.

The climax was yesterday when all the temple supporters and Go Roshi came for a ceremony and dinner, but the day before was zenkai, so trying to keep the whole place in order and the new snow all shovelled out was near miraculous. But it's over, and today I'm just taking it easy. A Swiss friend is going back soon and is having a big "do" at the Grand Hotel—an 8000-yen-a-head affair. It seemed a bit extravagant to me, but Jim insisted on paying for me, so I'll go mad tonight.

Scott, it's a pity you couldn't have been here to walk, too. As it was, this year I got even more publicity than before (the radio once, papers twice, and local and national TV four times), but they would have loved Scott. The bit I enjoyed the most but hadn't looked forward to at all was a TV current-affairs interview spot. It was in the studio and a bit awesome with all the cameras and mikes and things, but we really had a great laugh—even in Japanese. Everywhere I go now, strangers point at me and run out to shake hands. It's weird.

One of the gaijin who came up for takuhatsu, a Scotswoman, Allison, had reached one of those "life turning points," tried everything but was not satisfied, etc., etc. After a couple of late-night heart-to-hearters, she decided she wanted to try being a monk, at least for a couple of years. When she went back to Toshoji, she had her initial ceremony. She's supposed to come up and help me here next summer. I presumed I'd just continue here "as is," but I'll probably go back to Tokyo after Tetsugen-san's ceremony proclaiming him the head of Kannonji temple, probably in September. Allison phoned from Tokyo frantic that Go Roshi wanted her to come up immediately, and she wasn't sure if she wanted to be in such an isolated position. I still don't know her decision. However, apparently the monk who was translating for her didn't want to disappoint

Go Roshi so he made it sound as if she was more willing to come than she is. Anyway, Go Roshi came up here, full of plans for my remaining time. He wants me to do my remaining two ceremonies. (To do this I'd have to spend a period of time in Toshoji, so Allison's coming here would free me.) Then I'd be all official, registered at the head temple and qualified to head a temple, though not yet to teach.

Up to now we have our busy times here, then the calms while I recuperate. But Go Roshi wants me to help cover both temples and go back and forth between Toshoji and here as well as doing various ceremonies with him around the country. At the moment the schedule is March and early April in Toshoji, then back up to Kannonji, down to Kyushu in May, then maybe Nagano. Back to Tokyo for my ceremony in June, in July sesshin at Kannonji, then July obon [Buddhist All Saints Day Festival] *in Toshoji, August obon at Kannonji, etc. He says he wants to bring me around Japan as an example to others, but I'm seriously wondering if I can keep up the pace of this 72-year-old cancer patient. Anyway, I'm game to try.*

Up 'til now the only thing I've regretted about Kannonji was only being able to do dokusan once a month, but Go Roshi says that while we're together he'll do extra ones at noon and in the evening. It's very kind of him; it would be as often as sesshin. I'd certainly finish Hegikan Roku ["The Blue Cliff Record" book of koans] *and maybe the next book. He says when I leave he wants it to be with a certificate to teach, but that usually takes 10 years. It's unprecedented to be given one after 3 years (as it is for him to do all those private dokusans). I feel very touched but very unworthy. He only sees me at my busy times, when I've no choice but to do my best. Anyway, it's very exciting but completely depends on Allison.*

Mum, he seems to be taking his discussion with you seriously. He hasn't even jokingly suggested my staying on next year (even when one of the papers mistakenly printed that I'd stay 2 more years). I was wondering with all that activity how I'd work on my books. My novel is okay, as I've pretty much figured it out and it's just a matter of getting it down, which I could do when I get back, but the translation needs to be done here. We hadn't mentioned it to Go Roshi yet, so he stunned me when yesterday he announced to the supporters that all the contributions they'd made were going into an account he'll open in order to publish his books in English if I'd be good enough to translate them. So I've a busy few months ahead. Scott, I hope you won't be bored if you come over, because I won't be able to devote myself to you as totally as I'd like. Anyway, all of you take good care.

Very very much love, M.

WEDNESDAY, FEBRUARY 24

Overslept. Meditations not very good lately, but feel incredibly indefatigably happy. Still, should try to get more proficient in samadhi. Miko-san came and taught me about seika flower arranging. As always many presents. Dominique phoned; I will meet her tomorrow.

FEBRUARY 25

Morning meditation was good at the beginning and end. Even when not concentrating, I felt suffused by an incredible joy. It amazes me that such a physical thing—no supernatural gods interfering–as just sitting, maybe breathing a bit differently, can fill one with such elation. Did a million things at once and left early to meet Dominique. Talked in tiny, cozy, intimate cake shop. She worries so about nothing but has fantastic heart. Got her to agree to try zazen daily for 6 months. She always asks a million questions and explanations are useless. I spent a long time with Umezawa Sensei. He's deeply enlightened, sees everything as flowers. All existence in threes: shin, jin, tome/ past, present, future. He had that one koan but came to understand everything.

FEBRUARY 26

Tessai-san at hospital. No-one came; didn't get a ton done. Tessai has really changed, become much nicer.

Yesterday he actually did some cleaning. Today he brought me home a slice of cheesecake. Evening meditation drowsy.

FEBRUARY 27

Morning meditation awful, three quarters asleep. Must improve. How? Went to *Fukudo-ji [Happiness Hall Temple]* where Go Roshi was raised. His elder-brother-*deshi* [disciple] and family were there. The scenery was exquisite. Very cold. The stories of Go Roshi as a child clipclopping down the road in thin geta (no socks) through the wind and snow, crying from the pain, came alive. Of being awakened and beaten at 3 in the morning with snow on his futon. We also went to nearby Tendaiji, high on the mountain. Very remote and peaceful. Heavenly for training. Nice day. Night meditation good. Lately I always get sleepy about halfway through, so I took a break, had a cuppa and a bit of a read, then was able to continue well. I haven't solved the koan but had some samadhi. Around 11 o'clock, I heard strange laughing—howling like a woman's voice. Very eerie, but I presume it was owls or something.

FEBRUARY 28

Phew, time is flying. Morning meditation bad. Gion-chan was sleeping with me. In my semi-slumber I was loth to move her and got up late myself, 4:40. Got loads of work done. Fell asleep at 9.

MARCH 2

Morning meditation only okay. Allison came, it was nice to see her. We had a little celebration. Bad meditation.

MARCH 3

Go to dokusan but miss the bus, so we walked. It was a nice day; we did it in 80 minutes. Roshi says that in 30 years of training I'm the only one of his students who trains as if "*inochi o steru*" *["to abandon my very life"]*. I messed up the koan a bit, but it was generally okay. Home very late.

MARCH 4

Gidaji, flower-arranging. Home late.

MARCH 5

I'm a bit tired but have to do ookyo at home of dead neighbor. The woman, still in *nemaki [nightgown]*, could have been asleep except for purple ears and hanky on her face. Disconcerting. Her child lay on his stomach in *kotatsu [a quilted warmer]* and stared at the corpse on its futon. Relatives kept wiping her lips with water; it shone on her dead mouth. A single tulip, a candle in line so the stem and the stalk coincided, the flame rising from the base of the tulip. She had a cold that didn't get better, so they operated on her throat in the hospital and killed her. Forty-three years old.

March 6

Met Reiko-san and had a sumptuous lunch, then went to a magnificent flower-arranging exhibition.

It seems to me the difference between life and death is consciousness (even plants are conscious), and the difference between human and other life is self-consciousness. In Zen, the narrow subjectivity of consciousness is transcended, becomes pure subjectivity rather than relative subjectivity.

Allison is sick.

Sunday, March 7

Morning meditation mostly drowsing, but I solved the koan that had been annoying me. Go Roshi pulled a great one. When Kondo-san's people came looking for him, Go Roshi first tried to persuade them not to pursue him, then he pretended to give up, hid Kondo-san in the pre-fab, and had one of the monks pretend he'd run away from Toshoji. They then gave up but threatened that they'd be back in touch. Then someone stole Jean's money, and Go Roshi, suspecting Atchan, went prowling around in the dark to check on him. He fell and hurt his leg. He's sleepless with concern over the theft.

March 8

Allison is still quite sick. She went into hospital. They

say it's enteritis and give her pills that only make it worse. She's brave.

Toshoji, Tokyo
March 18, 1982

Dear Mum,

A huge package of books arrived from you the other day. This is the first moment I've had to write and thank you. I'm dying to launch into them. The Kadowaki one, "Zen and the Bible" looks particularly fascinating. Just leafing through it, the man seems very illumined and obviously has grasped and lived both worlds. I was extremely impressed with just the little I've read.

It seems to me that every day something happens and I say "Oh, I must tell Mum that," but now I don't know where to start.

My ceremony has been moved from June to April 25th. Go Roshi says he's not sure if he'll be alive in June, so he wants to do the ceremony as soon as possible. I'm going bats trying to learn all the stuff. It's old Japanese and has completely different tonality and pronunciation from regular conversational Japanese.

For a week I was doing ookyo at the different people's houses (just by myself I did about 70 houses). It was fascinating. The people around Morioka are really pretty much all of one type, but here (in the Shingawa section of Tokyo) I got much more of a cross-section, from modern, luxurious, western-style concrete, with plate glass and a dining-room table, to tiny, dark, second floor hovels. Some were weensy little garrets where, after stepping over boxes and up a two foot wide staircase, there would be a single room where a whole family lives in oriental harmony. The people were very good to me, and I was amazed at how broadminded they were. (How would you react if a young girl from Bombay dressed as a priest walked into St. Joseph's Church to offer Mass?) Quite apart from my being gaijin, most had never even seen a woman read ookyo before. It was, however, exhausting. I did a house an hour.

I got around by bicycle and have become adept at misreading Japanese maps. No one can come up with more original ways to get lost. Meanwhile Go Roshi was bombing around on his bike—you know, like the big, black, 2-wheeled armored tanks that the Irish police, down the bogs, use. Other mornings he'd be out at 5 o'clock when he had to catch the subway to a distant house. That part wouldn't be so bad, except that he's doing it on a sprained ankle which has now become extremely painful and swollen.

He got the sprained ankle while checking up on a young "delinquent" we had here who used to borrow money and get jarred over in the prefab every night (the little house where we stayed when you were here). But it is because of another fellow that we are in bad odour with the police here. The guy was from Morioka and had committed offenses that I'm sure any American policeman would smile at, but they were real shockers in Morioka. His mother was a wreck (her only beautiful boy—and he is gorgeous), so she begged Go Roshi to take him. She didn't mention that he was on parole and not allowed out of Morioka. The police caught up with him just after they found out about Kondo-san. (Remember the sweetheart of a monk who was always fixing you sandwiches?)

Anyway, the young man was a friend of Reiko-san (the temple mum, where I teach English), and his father was a monk, who re-married after Kondo-san's mother died. It was a classic Cinderella tale. The stepmother hated him, favoured her own son, whom she wanted to inherit the temple, rather than Kondo-san who, as eldest son, was in line for it. So she succeeded in making life miserable for him and in promoting her own son in the father's favour. Kondo-san, from young childhood, had to do most of the cooking and cleaning in the temple and sell newspapers after school. On the one afternoon a week he had free, he worked with handicapped kids. Well, after 20 years and no sign that things would improve, even Kondo-san was starting to get discouraged. Reiko-san stepped in and helped him to run away. (Imagine, 28 years old and having to run away from home, but such is temple life in Japan). It was summer. Bit by bit he smuggled out boxes of clothes, mostly winter ones, so that it would look as if he was going to Hokkaido. Reiko-san, as wife in a very prominent temple, was putting her neck on the block. They got him to Toshoji.

For a month the police didn't get wind of him. Then one of the dormitory students got stopped for drunken bicycling, and Kondo-san went to bail him out. They asked his name and birth-place. Not having a sly bone in his body, he 'fessed up. Explosion! His people came down for him (after many intense phone calls). Finally Go Roshi hid him in a cupboard and had another monk let on that he had run away from here, too. I don't know what will happen next, but the police have black-listed Toshoji. There's certainly never a dull minute here.

I've kind of adopted that poor mutt Guru (remember the one with the unearthly howls?). I never thought of myself as a dog person, but dogs are really great. They give you so much more of a reaction than cats.

I'm blasting through koans these days. I can scarcely keep up and seldom have time to prepare them properly, but Go Roshi figures that if he at least gives me the key to them, then I can digest them later. Phew! My head is spinning a bit.

A couple of days later . . . I'm very excited about the news that Scott is coming. I only wish he could have been here in time for my ceremony. We're busy preparing for sesshin. Right now I'm up on the roof mending futons. It's a beautiful sunny day, a change from the weather of late. It's so very pleasant sitting up here in the sun and wind, sewing, listening to the children playing in the streets below.

Today a woman from some Tokyo magazine came for an interview, and before I left Morioka, I did a long radio thing that was to be played in installments for a week. I wouldn't be surprised if Scott ends up on radio or TV or in some magazine. I haven't worked on my novel for weeks, but it's in the works. How's about Christmas in dear old dirty Dublin?

Much love, M.

TOSHOJI, TOKYO
APRIL 1982

Dear Mum,

Happy Easter! It's a glorious Easter Sunday here but without a bonnet in sight (in fact, only conspicuously bald heads). They'd give anything for Easter weather like this in Ireland—seems a shame to waste it on infidels.

Sesshin is over, and practice for my ceremony is in full swing. I'm going over, and over again, the same meaningless syllables *(ancient Japanese that even the Japanese don't understand). I have to do all the tonality and pronunciation in a peculiar oratorical style resembling the Kabuki narrators. It's going to be unusual anyway. . . .*

Scott, I'm as excited as can be that you're coming. For clothes, the young Japanese casual uniform is a track suit, though that may be hot in a Tokyo summer. You may want to ship back most of your baggage ahead, as we'll travel light in Thailand and India. My ideal is one of those weekender packs, a sleeping bag and rain poncho that can open into a ground sheet, a set of clothes on one's back, a set in the pack, and a light jumper or cardigan (maybe not necessary; I must check the likely weather). I don't believe in money belts. Everyone knows about them, and the pros all know how to relieve you of them. Get both large ($50.00) and small travellers' checks so you don't need to carry too many. Bring a nailbrush. Where do you want to go? Flights within southeast Asia are cheapest from Hong Kong, so we should start there, and flights back are cheapest from Thailand. Also, bring Lomotil in case of tummy problems. So start researching and dreaming, and let's have some fun.

Love, M.

March 30

Put out futons to air. Dug garden. Made oryoki. Six hours zazen. Nakamura read me koans on the floor by flashlight. First hint of any interest in me.

March 31

Changed address at *Yakuba [ward office]*. Preparing for sesshin. I feel an incredible joy, incredible energy. The koans are still hopeless.

> *Somewhere a door creaks*
> *I crane for a*
> *certain footstep.*

April 1-5

Sesshin. Kitchen great, I wasn't tired, it became the heart of the temple. Everyone streeled in in dribs and drabs if they needed a chat or a cry, an ookyo book, rice balls, a cup of tea, if their legs hurt or they had a headache or cold, if their kimono needed sewing or their rakusu, if their dokusan needed translation or if their address book had to be fished out of the toilet; they all came to the kitchen. Me and Kondo-san were the mother, Go Roshi the stern but beloved father. During their meals I'd lie down on the kitchen floor with my head on a rice sack, and a smile would creep across my face. We were very happy, worked very hard, and laughed very hard. My koans weren't great, I had scarcely time to prepare them. Still, Go Roshi says that of all his disciples I stand alone. Politically, we could never agree. I appreciate his points, and if everyone felt like him, as apparently they used to, it would be great. I doubt he'd ever appreciate my point.

APRIL 1

Allison and Mike got kensho. It was very beautiful to be with her then, but later she was disillusioned and depressed. She still doesn't really know she's Buddha. Mike had no expectations or disappointments.

APRIL 2

Kiguchi-obasan from Morioka had kensho. In zendo she could hear my voice doing ookyo (but I wasn't); then she was crying and got into the dokusan line. I was watching Namura suffering and failing dokusan, and Kiguchi was crying beside me. It became too much. I began to cry, too. She was deeply moved and had kensho. I ran downstairs, collapsed in a heap in the corner by my rice bag, sobbing uncontrollably. They were all suffering so. Stuart came in, was shocked and comforting. I left meals outside Namura-san's door. He wasn't getting kensho, and I was afraid it might bother him to think I was watching. He tried with his heart and soul, and mine, but he didn't get kensho. Even in the kitchen I'd call "Mu, mu," to him, but my concentration was bad. He seems sad these days, hasn't been doing zazen.

I'd like to reach out to him, but he often seems strained in my presence.

Go Roshi was an inspiration. His leg is still dreadful, but he struggled to sit on it. I begged him to use a chair but he refused. The leg has swollen to twice its size. In dokusan, he was continually shifting because of the pain of sitting long hours on it. This sesshin I was right weepy. Tears just streamed down my face, touched that he'd do this for us, pained to see him. He says I'm not to go back to Kannonji.

APRIL 7

Roshi went to Morioka, Yamaguchi goes home for a couple of days. Drizzle day, mostly sewing.

APRIL 8

Count Basie concert with Yuriko and Hiroshi. Roshi still in Morioka. I knocked down an old shed. Went for a drive with Izaki-san. It was pathetic. Surrounded by concrete warehouses, a towering official with a walkie-talkie, Izaki-san looked up at him and said, "We just want to see the sea." A gull circled overhead. "Impossible." We drove for ages and finally saw a bit of the sea by the airport. I talked to Namura a bit, but he seems very cold. He hasn't seemed well since sesshin. In torrential rains in the afternoon, met Roshi at the station. Yen phoned, Allison frantic that I won't be returning to Kannonji.

APRIL 10

I chopped up the shed and put the wood away. Put ashes on the garden. My practice for *Hossenshiki [koan graduation ceremony]* not very good. I'm sleeping four and a half hours with no problems. Feel good.

APRIL 13

I decided to approach Namura. He looked so mopish and depressed. He hadn't been doing zazen in zendo. But I came on like a bulldozer. He didn't know how to react. I asked if he was okay, and he said he didn't seem right. Then, Japanese style, he started apologizing. I ranted and raved about the Japanese repressing their feelings, etc.

A new American woman, Jocelyn Ford, entered. Seems she may be serious.

Izaki brings me cheesecake.

APRIL 15

I put mondo to Go Roshi.

"The stone that is now preaching the Dharma, is it living or dead?"

He said "*Isshi, konna ishi?*" ["*Stone, this stone?*"], indicating.

I said "Hai."

He said "I don't know," then laughing, "ask the stone."

I said, "I am asking the stone." We were both laughing.

He said, "I'm not a stone. I'm Ban Tetsugyu," and we both dissolved into laughter.

Jiko-san came, back from India.

Bad zazen, very sleepy, disorganized. Couldn't do dokusan in the morning. Pouring rain.

APRIL 17

Abe says he'll help, and I have written to various people asking them to visit Allison.

Actually had a five minute conversation with Namura. Since my outburst, he seems in much better humour. I don't know if there's a connection.

In the evening went to zenkai with Go Roshi. Maezumi Roshi was there. Seems good. The whole thing was great fun. Roshi was in a very good humor. We went by subway with Maezumi Roshi asking Go Roshi, "Where's your car?" Go Roshi wouldn't let either of us carry his bag, so Maezumi shared it with him. They fought like little boys going down the street in the dark, and finally both carried the minuscule briefcase. I walked behind in undignified convulsions of laughter. Roshis!

APRIL 18

It was Go Roshi's grandchild's birthday. They invited me over. I was very touched.

Allison phoned, she's not getting on with Tetsugen.

I went to see Kiguchi-san. His mother was returning in the morning, and I wanted to stay and give her an obento. Turned out it was Kiguchi's birthday too, and Namura was there. I left to phone Allison, planning to come right back. He left.

Allison was asleep, but I asked Tetsugen to give her free time each week. He didn't seem to mind. Sounded good.

I felt disappointed that Namura was gone and annoyed with myself for being disappointed. Zazen was bad, so I went up on the roof. It was getting late, and Namura's laundry was out, so I was putting it away just as he came for it. We talked for a long while. It was nice, but when Izaki and Kiguchi appeared, Namura scarpered.

Kondo is a sweetheart, brought me an eclair.

APRIL 19

I decided to try three hours sleep. I was exhausted. I tried reading the paper, next thing I remember it was 4 o'clock and Go Roshi was knocking on the door, calling me to dokusan. Things went wrong all day. Really seemed jinxed. I suggested to Roshi that Gen go to Nagano, Mio to Toshoji, and Allison to Kannonji. He said he wanted me to marry a Japanese man and run one of the temples. He's given that a rest for a while. Another goof: I tried to give Kiguchi a late birthday present, poised it atop his window ledge, and it fell. Highly breakable. It was Roshi's 33rd wedding anniversary.

April 20

Go Roshi stunned me in dokusan. I'd been thinking about Namura being seven years younger than me, and that really this attraction is absurd, when Go Roshi told me the story of the woman who jumped into the toilet to save the cat. From all the priests she had picked out the best one, the one most serious about training, as she herself had been. The one she chose was seven years younger than herself. Roshi looked at me meaningfully. "I want you to follow her, that is, choose for yourself."

My Hossenshiki *renshu* [*practice*] is 120 percent thanks to Abe-san, who drills me very kindly.

The funny, drunken former tenzo came back again. He sat with his sandals outside the gate, heaving big sighs. He became a bit violent.

April 21

Go Roshi is pushing me hard to stay in Japan and become his successor. I feel disoriented. All my previous principles, goals, opinions seem totally changed. Whether I'm here or in Ireland, married or not, none of it seems a big deal. It seems I should assent and truly throw my life away for training. Mum would be upset. In the real world, Roshi's and my ideas are so different. But it seems I have no criteria left by which to make a decision. Anything is okay. It's a strange feeling, not a problem, but definitely disorientating.

I did *insatsu* [*printing*] in the evening, with the rain falling.

Roshi said my interpretation of the koan was deeper than the koan. Then he thanked me. I was touched.

Allison phoned again; it's hard for her.

April 22

I planted flowers, weeded, did insatsu, sewed. I love all the people in Toshoji, each and every one of them. They're all excellent, not a bad apple in the bunch.

April 25

My ceremony.

I practiced too hard the day before so my voice was not at its best but was okay. Wonderful day. I had prepared a good speech, but when asked to speak, could only burst out crying. I got very emotional and kept bowing and thanking people. (I spent all my money in a frenzy of gratitude, buying things for everyone.) Many beautiful gifts to me; I was extremely moved.

In the evening we had my party. Kondo-san hurt his back, so I had to do all the cooking. Tired. Up at 2:30, great energy in hossenshiki, then no break. Cook and clean.

They all dedicated songs to me. Yamaguchi was roaring, looked as if his blood vessels would pop, thumping his leg. Izaki, swaying, romantic, asked Namura for a song, but Namura said he couldn't sing. Later he stood up shouting, "Everyone's done a song for Mora; only I haven't because I can't sing." So he did a wild, impassioned, cheerleading type of thing, punching the air, creating dazzlers, screaming my name. I wanted to run to him.

Later I couldn't meditate for thinking of him, so I went to the roof. Kondo-san was lying on his back, drunk, singing powerfully to the stars. He then calls into the night: "Mora-san, I made a mistake (in the ceremony). Sorry." He's so pure, beautiful. I sat on the steps. I was a bit worried about Kiguchi, so I headed that way with the dog, met Izaki, Namura, and friends going to the baths. I asked directions to the park; Namura didn't show me the way.

April 26

Poor Kondo-san, still maimed. Abe-san is doing massages and needles. I am doing the kitchen.

April 27

Namura is definitely not interested, so to hell with it. I'll just forget about him.

I spent hours getting Roshi's *tabi* [socks] dry by the morning, then he didn't wear them.

There is nothing dead. Everything alive is in movement, if only in time.

May 1-5

Did sesshin in traditional temple in Kyushu. Allison

shaved her head. Go Roshi was happy. Her poor legs gave her agony. We ate and slept in zendo. I made many mistakes in protocol, but Tetsumon-san helped me.

It was the best sesshin I'd ever experienced. I had two minor awakenings. On the second day, in dokusan line, I realized–really experienced– *"ten ni mo chi ni mo tada ware hitori."* [*"In heaven and earth, there is but I, myself."*] That "ware hitori" includes everything.

Later, during teisho, I felt such intense gratitude toward Go Roshi, I could only cry. I cried for about an hour and a half.

On the fourth day, my awakening began in the corridor and became intense while I was eating. Everything is perfect. Everything is enlightening, just as it is by virtue of being. As it is, it is *narikiteru* [*totally being*], even *bonpu* [*the mundane unenlightened state*] is narikiteru bonpu. It was revelation, the perfection within the imperfection. Many times Go Roshi's words of remonstrance penetrated to my very core. "Is there even one of you truly narikiteru?" I'm not.

At the end, Hukokuji's Roshi made a speech and referred to the fact that, like Dogen Zenji, I hadn't slept lying down for a thousand days. I was so ashamed and also inspired to do better during the final *Shiku Seigan Mon* [*Four Vows*]. I was weeping again, intensely grateful to have the opportunity to experience this sesshin.

I forgot about Namura. I must just do good training, no distractions.

Tetsumon-san made a weird speech. He likes me (loves me, he says) but is justifiably put out by Roshi's exaggerations of my worth and his condemnation of the Japanese. I wish Roshi wouldn't do it.

Allison is to come to Toshoji in July; I wonder how Namura will feel. People have started doing zazen. At first it was only me, now there are five of us in the evenings.

I feel ecstatically happy. It's a gorgeous May, warm and breezy. I love the world.

May 14

Last night I stayed up late talking with Namura—very good, very open, spontaneous, and relaxed. I realized many things. I grew to like him more, and I feel closer to him, but am put off him as a man. He's still too young. I'd hate to either dominate or mother him, as would be inevitable. That leaves me freer to concentrate on training. But he's a wonderful person.

Go Roshi returned. He seemed tired but strong.

May 15

Reiko-san and Megumi came to visit. I was very happy. Megumi is unsure about her future. (A Morioka woman who was apparently moved to tears to see me in takuhatsu, wants me to help her son tread the right road, return to school, etc. These are strange cases. I feel wilder than the kids.)

I have started cleaning the toilets again at 3 o'clock in the morning. Three hours' sleep. I am pretty much asleep sitting up, but still bad.

The weather threatens rain, but it is beautiful.

TOSHOJI, TOKYO
MAY 17, 1982

Dear Kate,

. . . Just had a phone call from Jane. Nearly dropped. It's May 17, I wished her happy birthday, she said it wasn't her birthday. Beginning to wonder if I had 2 sister Janes or was going soft in the head. It's still yesterday there (and Go Roshi always says the past doesn't exist).

It's sunny. I'm watching the beans grow. It's a happy, peaceful day, neighborhood. People all doing Oriental neighborhoodsy things, and the kids are feeding shoes to our dog, who is called Guru, and kept on a chain. This morning we did a funeral for a cat. I became an official female priest on Ruth's birthday. I'm Soshin osho now.

The funeral people brought us a big feed of sashimi in thanks. Seems appropriate to get raw fish for burying a cat.

I'm sitting in May sunshine and winds overlooking Tokyo. If it was a clear day, I could see Mt. Fuji, but it's not, so I can't. I've been sitting up here mending Go Roshi's patches. He's been wearing this robe for 50 years, so I'm putting patches on the patches, and it's all fraying in my hands and these heavenly May winds. So I'm taking a break and writing to you, without much to say.

Days fly past, cleaning and sitting and having a laugh. It's nice living with people again. All good people, but like any bunch living in a small space, many undercurrents. The Japanese aren't big on face-to-face encounters, etc., yet everyone just seems to know what's afoot. I've shocked more than one by saying the unsaid, out.

Go Roshi is good. Had planned to die this year. It's the year of the dog; he was born in the year of the dog, so he wanted to have a big bash and pass on. But his book's been delayed, and half the text has gone amissing, so he's putting off his retirement.

★

Another day. It's three in the morning. I've just finished washing all the toilets, pulled up the poles, and opened the gates, put out the offertory box and the outside offerings. Some drunks are staggering home, and I still don't feel quite coherent but reckon you've been waiting quite a while for an answer.

I guess the most exciting thing that's happened to me lately is the sesshin in Kyushu. Kate, it was great. I got to just be a participant. No cooking, serving or patrolling, but loads of zazen. Anyway had a couple of real breakthroughs. Very overwhelming, tears and laughter and a long sit in a pebble garden. Now they seem tenuous. Old habits die hard but the experiences are there, I now really know what I had theretofore assented to as being true. Anyway excellent, though as excitement it probably seems boring in the context of what you're doing. (Well, to hell with contexts.) . . . Kate, I have to go. Write again.

Take care, M.

MAY 18

The clock stopped, and the dog broke a bag of garbage. I saw both and took care of neither. Funbetsu—I'll do it later. I haven't the responsibility here.

MAY 19

I'm making myself do jobs when I'm willing to turn a blind eye. Made juice, sewed clothes on the roof. I began work on the *Mumonkan* [*"Gateless Gate," a book of koans*] translation again.

MAY 21

I had an incredibly wonderful walk with the dog through the streets. They were playing music; I wanted to dance. A mother watched her child eat pink ice cream. The summer plastic festoons have gone up, silver and blue. The streets seemed to be in festival. Smells of soba. Vegetable stalls. Old man on a bicycle. Young lovers not holding hands.

Ichigawa-san was afraid to sleep in her room, so we traded. Had a laugh. I heard funny noises and thought Namura was playing tricks on me. He'll be a fine man, but not right for me. Nice to really know it and nice that he's relaxed with me. The dormitory students have been coming down with things. I like mothering them. Everyone takes care of me in so many ways—fixing me treats, giving me papers, helping me with my koans, shaving my head. They're all patient, kind. We love one another beyond nationality or sex.

I have been tired for the last couple of days, almost no sleep. I am ashamed, though, of my shoddy efforts. I read about the old masters, bow to the living Buddha before me in dokusan, and try, but I am still very far from *risshin* [*success*], from narikiteru.

It was a rainy day, very nice. Greens intense, pink roses.

May 23

Jim and Dominique are in town. I stood bald under the *Star Wars* sign in Ueno Park. Many stares in the razzle-dazzle of the night. I met Jim's mum, her birthday is the same as mine.

May 24

My birthday. Paul sends instant birthday kit from Dublin: Guinness, cake, and tapes. We have a hell of a party, dancing on the roof. Lovely gifts. Crazy night. Tired next day.

May 26

In the morning I felt exhausted to my bones. I feel I will surely collapse, I have reached some kind of limit, breaking point. I wanted to sleep 24 hours. I will surely collapse in sesshin. The tiredness has accumulated. Sleep after breakfast for an hour. During the morning the tiredness falls away. I can scarcely believe it. At lunch I feel alert enough to write letters. Really strange. My shoulders feel tight, but my body no longer seems tired either. (Izaki-san, so funny, doing zazen he feels strength he says came from me, sitting opposite.)

June 6

We had sesshin from June 1-5. Time flew. Allison and I in the kitchen. She's moody but a very big help. Kondo-san has kensho. I'm delighted. Also Ichigawa-san and a German, Helmut. I was translating for four people. Very busy, often began at 3:00-3:30, clean toilets, work all day.

June 8

We went to the park, danced barefoot. Kikuchi and Izaki-san played the guitar and sang. In the distance we could hear a baritone and flute player. We raced bikes home. I fell asleep in zendo.

June 10

Namura's folks came, worried about him. Made us promise not to tell.

June 12

Galli-san phones, trying to come to sesshin. No expectations or anxiety. I can't imagine. His voice was good. I am working on *Tetsugyushi* [*Go Roshi's book*] and Mumonkan. In the evening I met Namura on the roof. The air was heavenly. We had a good chat, open. I told him some of the problems I had at the age of 20; he seemed eased.

June 13

Izaki-san came back, did some Mumonkon. I was starving. Kondo-san is doing the wedding arrangements. I cook for two ceremonies. Did a fantastic zazen on the rooftop.

June 14

For the first time since he was sick, Namura did ookyo the energetic way he used to. I'm delighted.

June 18

I begin *Denpo-shiki* [*transmission ceremony*]. Three thousand full bows. Have one week to do it in. For the first ten minutes or so it felt good. Breathing deep from the hara, "*Namu san ze sho bu(tsu)*" ["*Homage to all the buddhas of the Three Worlds*"] again and again. Up and down, head bowing, blood rushing to the head, hyperventilating. Then I began to feel dreadful. Everything hurt, breathing, legs, stomach, dizzy. Kondo and Izaki gave me treats. I continued, barely took breaks. Was drenched in sweat. I began to lose awareness, felt there was a noise, a movement, vague sustained awareness of heat, but no "I." If I stopped, the pain in my legs was excruciating, but doing it again, I became unaware of them. Fifty wooden chopsticks from side to side. I finished 3036 the second day. Everyone was incredulous. Do banka, then straight out to zenkai. I was falling asleep there. The stairs were hell.

June 20

Father's Day.

Up early. Legs dreadful.

I have my Denpo-shiki. Very moving. Early in the morning, 50 bows. I do *doshi* [*officiate*]. Hardly notice my legs. I have to concentrate. I can scarcely do all the bows. We bow together. Abe-san attends. Go Roshi removes my *okesa* [*outermost robe of the fully ordained*] and gives me a gorgeous okesa. When it finishes, I cry more.

I sneak into his room and leave pens, goodies, a card, and roses.

June 22

Usha, an Indian Hindu, comes for the night. She's a very wonderful, intelligent, unusual woman. I'll visit her again.

June 24

I spent the day getting photocopies. I lost and found my dokusan notebook. Izaki was incredibly kind to me.

June 25

I returned a book to the Zenkai temple. There was a

letter from home. I phoned Scott's host family to let them know when he would arrive.

TOSHOJI, TOKYO
JUNE 1982

Dear Mum,

. . . Hope Scott comes soon, as the 10th of July until the 6th of August will be hectic for me with the summer equinox sutras. I have to do 80 houses in 5 days, then race up to Kannonji and get the place ready for sesshin, then do sesshin, rush back here to prepare for the August sesshin, cater that (sweltering Tokyo in August). So anyway, I hope he comes soon. Did you get my letter telling you how Paul, from Ireland, managed to give me a brilliant birthday party? On Go Roshi's birthday he phoned from London. He said he had a great time in Dublin. . . . I've been working every day on translating Go Roshi's book. It's very hard. When I go back to Ireland, I want to study Japanese seriously. In order for proper Zen (not "pop Zen") to take root in the West, there are a lot of vital

texts that simply must be translated. All present translations are really inadequate. I'll explain another time. I'm not crazy about translation work, but it has to be done, so . . .

Koan study is proceeding at a dizzying pace. Quite a few foreigners are coming these days, so I translate all their dokusans. This is a great opportunity for me because I see again and again how to deal with beginners and to adapt one's approach and one's answer to the needs of the person. So I'm thriving, but by October will be ready for a break. . . .

Love, M.

TOSHOJI, TOKYO
JULY 4, 1982

Dear Okachan [Mum],

Well, your son has safely arrived and quickly acclimatized. There was an accident on the runway, so his plane had to circle overhead for ages. I was there at 3:30. He finally arrived at 8:10. It gave me plenty of time to talk with his host family. When he arrived, they recognized him; I didn't. I insisted that grown-up young man wasn't Scott. Like Peter, I denied him three times before it finally hit me that it might indeed be my brother. He's much changed, very likeable. The poor kid had been awake for 28 hours

but managed in a foreign culture to be very gracious, helpful, atten-
tive, and extremely positive. Really he was delighted by everything.
He tucked right into the raw fish with relish, likes his family very
much, and when he finally got to go to bed, he wanted to unpack
and put away everything from his suitcase first, so as not to be
messy! Really, I was very impressed with the way he only saw the
good side of everything and made a real effort (though it seemed
effortless). But I can't get over how very American he seems.

His family let me spend the night there. They are lovely. The
father is gentle, with smiling eyes, very intrigued by Scott. He only
knows how to say "thank you" in English.

Scott took to the whole thing like a fish to water. No awk-
wardness, as if he'd been in Japan for years. He seemed to know all
the right things to do, how to hold his glass, to pour for others, how
to sit politely, etc.

The mother is delightful—one of those super duper Japanese
housewife types. She had worried awfully about Scott coming, afraid
he'd be too tall for the futons, etc. She actually lost weight worrying.
The older son is 24, has spent over a year in the States, so speaks
fluent English and understands how it is to be away from home and
in a strange culture. The girl's English is good, though slow. She's
outgoing and fun. They've arranged for Scott to attend her school.
All the girls there are dying to meet him. In short, things got off to a
very nice start.

Scott wants to give sesshin a try, though he'll miss the Kannonji one on account of school. It's a pity. I wanted him to meet all the folks up there. We were both dismayed by our mutual dates. The very earliest I can leave (doing all my packing, buying, goodbyes before sesshin) would be October 7th. Scott feels he must be back at school by mid-October.

A wonderful Indian woman came to stay here recently. She's 50, single, a lecturer in psychology, and the student of an Indian guru. She has a house and servants on the Ganges. We got on extraordinarily well, and she invited me to come and stay as long as I wanted. In October there's a festival of lights and one of good and evil that she wants to show me. She says that October is most pleasant and she'll take me to various places of Buddhist interest as well as a visit to her ashram in the mountains. I wish there were some way that Scott could work things to come with me. I think I'd really enjoy his company.

Love, M.

TOSHOJI, TOKYO
JULY 16, 1982

Dear Mum,

. . . We are into obon now and suddenly two 69-year-old parishioners passed away. Remember, that involves wake, service at

home, one at temple, one at crematorium, and one at the grave.
We're going bonky. One of the dormitory students who has been
growing out his hair came home last night after a few drinks, merry,
singing, and rubbing his new hair, only to be told that we're desper-
ately short of priests. Would he mind shaving? God love him. Not a
grumble, just where are the clippers? Today I do ookyo from 8 in the
morning 'til 7 at night, then out to the wake. I hope someone feeds
me. Will write when there's more time. . . .

Love, M.

SEPTEMBER 1982

Dear Mum,

. . . We can't get info here in Tokyo on flights back to the
States from Thailand (the bargain ones) for Scott, so we'll wait 'til
we get to Thailand and then see what the story is there.

[Later] I've been having terrible trouble cashing our dollar
checks. Don't know how the Japanese handle international banking
at all. It's unfortunate that all this coincides with ohigan. *I'm unbe-*
lievably busy. (It's now 3:37 in the morning, and I'm stealing time
between jobs to write this.) It looks, however, as if the checks will
pass through by Monday.

I tried to contact Sr. Ruth Sheils, but our schedules didn't fit
well enough so we could meet, but we had a very nice long phone

chat. She's a very interesting and intelligent woman and will look me up in Ireland next summer. She told me a lot about Sacred Heart, Tokyo, and it sounds excellent.

    Days and days later: We've had ohigan, then a sesshin, in between my trying to organize packing, posting, visas, shopping, money, goodbyes—am totally exhausted, but it's almost over. The reason this took so infernally long was that I was waiting for definite news on our travel funds. It was hell. Anyway, I must post this NOW or not at all.

    Sorry! You can't imagine how busy things are. Will write.

                               Love, M.

EPILOGUE

In October of 1982, Maura finally set out to return to the West. Before going to Ireland, however, she planned to tour for two months in southeast Asia, then spend Christmas with her family in Maine. The temple people didn't want her to leave, but the fact that I was due back in school by mid-October gave a good reason for our early October departure from Japan.

On the flight from Tokyo to Bangkok, we met a charming Hong Kong woman who invited us to stay in her apartment in that city for a few days. So we explored Hong Kong and then took an overnight trip to Macao. Hotel rooms were too expensive there, so we spent the night on a huge rock that jutted out from a wall in Macao. We caught up on our sleep next day on a bus trip through the Chinese countryside, then back to Hong Kong.

Next we flew to Bangkok where we stayed several days at a guest house owned by the Devahastin family, Thai friends whom we had known in Dublin. Here Maura arranged the itinerary for her Asian journey, which was to start with a bus trip to the ancient capital of Thailand in the north, Chiang Mai. She was one of the last passengers to board the bus for the overnight trip so she sat at the front near the driver. When he fell asleep near dawn the bus went off the road killing Maura, the driver, and two other passengers. Although her passport and journal were stolen with her luggage, the police were able to identify her by means of a ticket stub they found in the pocket-like sleeve of her monk's robe. On October 23rd, I received the phone call from the U.S. State Department informing us of the accident. The consul at Chiang Mai arranged for the return of her remains after the cremation at Lapsang.

Maura's ashes are interred beside her father's in Mt. Hope cemetery in Lewiston, Maine.

—Scott O'Halloran

[A letter of condolence from Tetsugyu Ban to
the O'Halloran family]

 On December 8th, 1979, Maura O'Halloran
joined Toshoji Doairyo, and we had a Tokudo
Ceremony on December 10th. Her Tokudo
name was Daigo Soshin Hikyuni. She began her
vigorous training from that day.

On January 5th, 1980, at 6:30 A.M., she left Ueno
Station to the Kannonji in Yahabacho, Iwate-ken, with Sato
Jiko and Dote Tessen. For thirty days, from January 6th, she
trained in strict "Kan-Shugyo" (training in the freezing
cold). It was -20°C weather in Morioka where she had her
training. She returned to Toshoji on February 6th.

When I was ten, I had my Tokudo Ceremony at
Fukuzo-ji in Johoji, Iwateken. My master Fuchizawa Chiaki
said, "Zen monks must work 20 hours, and 3 hours for sleep
every day." Maura did exactly that.

Our grand master Dogen went to China and to the
Tendo mountain for one thousand days, working hard all day,
he sat for meditation at night. He slept two or three hours in
the sitting position. Maura did the same. She was the modern Dogen.

There was a spring training at Kannonji from May 2nd
for five days. Maura reached her enlightenment on the first
day. She went in for meditations twice, three times a day, and
solved all three thousand koans. We had her Hishinsai (graduation ceremony) on August 7th, 1982.

298

She requested to become a Tenzo for the fall training, starting from October 1st. Her wish was granted. She completed her circle and left Narita airport on October 9th.

I received an international telegram on October 25th, 8:00 P.M., which said Maura had died of accidents in Thailand on 24th. . . .

She had achieved what took the Shakuson [Shakyamuni Buddha] 80 years in twenty-seven years. She was able to graduate Dogen's thousand-day training. Then she left this life immediately to start the salvation of the masses in the next life! Has anyone known such a courageously hard working Buddha as Maura? I cannot possibly express my astonishment.

—Ban Tetsugyu
October 27, 11:00 P.M. as
I watch the eleventh day moon.

Maura Kannon (A brief history)

Miss Maura O'Halloran from Ireland.

*On the 10th of October in the 54th year of Showa [1979], at
Toshoji Temple she became a nun and completed 1,000 days of continuous
Zen practice at Toshoji and Kannonji Temples. Her daily practice included
three hours of sleeping in the zazen position and twenty hours of devotion
to her studies in order to attain salvation not only for herself but also for all
people.*

*On the 7th of August in the 57th year of Showa [1982], she was
conferred an authorized certificate of "Enlightenment Achieved."*

*On the 22nd of October, on her way back to Ireland, at Chiang
Mai, Thailand, by some traffic accident her life ended at the age of twenty-
seven.*

*She is given the posthumous name of "Great Enlightened Lady, of the
same heart and mind as the Great Teacher Buddha." Miss Maura has been a
real incarnation of Kannon Bosatsu to be loved and respected forever.*

*We dedicate the Maura Kannon Statue here to her extraordinary
memory.*

*Nirvana Day [February 15th] in the 58th year of Showa [1983],
by Tetsu-gyu So-in, founder of Kannonji Temple.*

—translated by Shiro Tachibana

301

Afterword

The life and death of Maura "Soshin" O'Halloran became known to me one late spring afternoon in 1987, during a tea break at a Soto Zen monastery in western Japan. I had recently been sent from our women's monastery on the Pacific side to be, as it turned out, the one American female monk among 28 Japanese male monks for four years of teachers' training. On a day after I had been there several weeks, Tessai-san, a senior monk, quietly related the story of his Irish-American Dharma sister, "Maura-san." Deeply touched to hear of her selfless practice, I asked him for a photograph of her. Although she had not been in my lineage, I wished to honor, with a daily offering of incense, the memory of an American sister in the Dharma, whose understanding would have been of so much help to others. Although there is a growing number of western female monks who have become fully transmitted Dharma teachers and did all or most of their Soto Zen training in Japan, at the time of Maura's transmission only two had preceded her.

Shortly after I returned to America, an article came to my attention from the *Commonweal* magazine, written by Ruth O'Halloran, containing excerpts from her daughter Maura's journals. When I read for myself the depth of Maura's realization, I began a correspondence with her mother. Before long, I received a copy of the full manuscript for a book that Mrs. O'Halloran had built around the journals that Maura had sent back home before her departure. Through the work of Mrs. O'Halloran, and through this "record of a pure heart" (one variation of a translation for "Soshin," her daughter's Dharma name), Maura's realization and practice are available to others as her teaching.

The structure of Maura's monastic Zen practice supported a "waking up" or enlightenment through intense meditation, known as zazen, for long hours in natural temperatures, full-voice chanting, sustaining oneself on the minimum necessary sleep and food, and working single-mindedly under the guidance of a master, or Roshi. Maura says her Roshi is delighted that she is not used to the cold, for it is better training—"When we sing, we see our breath." Getting up early is hard for her, so she gets up earlier yet—there is "the time of lucidity that comes after the tiredness"; "tiredness drains the discerning mind."

There are other rigors of monastic life, cooking, cleaning, sweeping, and cleaning some more. At first, Maura doesn't "get" it. Early on, she mentions the "stupid" menial cleaning and with no enlightenment. Later she can say, "The cleaning will be fine, Takuhatsu will be fine." One by one, the things she fears and dreads become acceptable.

In the early stages of training, nearly everyone comes down with one form or another of malnutrition, to which the body eventually adapts. It is often then that a better balance between body and spirit takes place. While Zen cooking contains many elements of the macrobiotic diet, it is not based on the idea of "health food" alone; it is "pure food," food donated and prepared with a pure spirit, but not necessarily nutritionally complete.

When Buddhism was brought to cold countries, famine often meant that much of the populace had nothing to eat themselves, much less to donate, and Zen monks could not be expected to live solely on alms. Zen practice was therefore speeded up in order for the monks to fit in the hours necessary to cultivate the fields and grow their own food. Consequently, not a morsel of food, a grain of rice, is ever wasted. Although the Tenzo monk, or cook, will often cut carrots and other vegetables into attractive designs for the noon meal (as Maura's assistant was doing), all leftovers, anything edible remaining from lunch, including the rims and tips of the carrots, are chopped up finely and made into a leftover rice and vegetable porridge for the evening's "non-meal." Maura is cautioned by her Roshi not to be different from the others, ". . . I eat fish for lunch because I eat what's given me."

Maura was assigned the role of Tenzo monk, which in the Soto Zen tradition is second only to that of the head of the temple because the Tenzo maintains the health of everyone else. Closely following in importance is the role of the Enju, or garden caretaker, which Maura also performed. His or her boss is Providence, and it is the fruits of the gardener's labors that, outside of alms and donations from the parishioners, supply the Tenzo. Maura planted vegetables, built compost retainers, made new beds, even hauled logs for borders alone on a wheelbarrow, and felt "at peace with dirt and wriggling things worth not more nor less than I." Maura carried out both these duties with full body and mind.

The ceaseless hard work, the spending of oneself, was not something outside of Maura. Doing what needs to be done, selflessly and singlemindedly, can be called a polishing of the heart, and it is from this that solid Zen practitioners appear to shine. Maura speaks of the radiant light that emanates from her Roshi, but it is she who shines and begins to take on a new appearance, seeming younger and more vibrant as her practice grows. And as her practice grows, her deep understanding becomes more and more apparent. She writes, "I want to live [my life] for other people. What else is there to do with it? . . . It's as if to give myself is all I can do as the flower has no choice but to blossom. . . . So I must go deeper and deeper and work hard, no longer for me, but for everyone I can help." Maura-san has come to understand that practice itself is enlightenment.

A central element of Maura's Zen training is takuhatsu, or begging. The important spiritual practice of this going out to receive alms food once pervaded all Buddhist countries. Today in some Theravadin countries, monks still make the alms rounds with their begging bowls to the homes of lay followers in their area for the monks' once-a-day meal. In Mahayana countries such as Japan, offerings of uncooked rice and vegetables are more often the rule, especially at harvest time. Both male and female monks carry tubular cloth for holding rice and go from house to house to receive the offering. The rice is poured into one end of the cloth, which is tied shut, balanced on the shoulders, and carried on to the next house. Full, the sack can weigh 40 pounds. Most of the year, however, offerings are monetary. Kangyo, the practice of begging in the cold, further deepened Maura's practice by making her experience the direst circumstances. The monks walk with bare fingers, holding a Buddha bowl in one hand, and a bell with a cloth-wrapped handle (so the fingers don't freeze to the metal) in the other. The only time the arms are lowered below elbow level is when receiving an offering. In summer, monks try not to prance in place as the heat of the asphalt pierces their straw sandals. In winter, straw sandals are soaked in the first steps to the monastery gate, and it is the continuous pace and the deep breathing for the chanting that warm our bodies.

The first winter, Maura follows the other monks light-heartedly, comparing the chanting on the way to "Christmas caroling every day." She cannot notice then that the mood of her Dharma brothers is that of preparation for the annual challenge, even when they solemnly bring her bandages for her symbolic "wounds." The second year, she is actually looking forward to it, "Sometimes you could actually feel an energy of givingness and purity from the people and I'd feed off it, it surging through me, my voice becoming loud and untiring." Going deeply into the practice of alms rounds in the snow, monks like Maura have no "me." It is the chanting that chants.

In the first winter, Maura speaks of the blessing she cannot give after each donation is made. Perhaps she had not yet been able to memorize the gatha in Japanese meaning, "Two offerings of materials and teachings. Virtue is boundless. Offering Wisdom—Dana Paramitsu is perfectly achieved." Takuhatsu is a mutual exchange, face to face, of spiritual and material. The sight of monks, heads down, the umbrella-like straw hat aimed against the driving snow, is an inspiration to their donors to persevere likewise with the problem in their own daily lives. And for monks, going each day is the lesson of humility that, without donors, a monk cannot exist. It is itself significant that by her third year, the local villagers considered it an honor to donate alms to Maura during takuhatsu.

O-Higan and O-Bon are two of the most important and busiest Buddhist events on the calendar. The word "higan" means "the other shore," or "Nirvana," the opposite of "shigan" or "this shore of life and death." The O-Higan E is a week of Buddhist services and sutra reading for the deceased in parishioners' families, the middle day of which is the equinox, either vernal or autumnal. O-Bon is the Japanese word for the Sanskrit term "Ullambana," which means "rescue from the torment of hanging upside down in hell." It is observed on the 15th day of the seventh month. In metropolises like Tokyo, it occurs in July, following the Julian calendar; in the countryside, the lunar calendar is followed, making O-Bon one month later. Sutras are recited by a monk in parishioners' homes, in front of the Butsudan, or family Buddhist altar, in order to soothe the torments of the deceased in the lower realms of existence. The story behind this practice is that the Buddha's disciple, Maudgalyayana, saw with his "divine eye" that his mother had been reborn as a hungry ghost and wanted to save her. The Buddha said that only the combined efforts of all Buddhist monks could ease the sufferings of the tormented; thus, sutras were recited and offerings were made to liberate them. The story teaches the importance of caring for our ancestors and family members, and the transference of merit to those we love.

The sutra recitations of O-Bon and O-Higan are not only for the repose of the deceased, but for the spiritual benefit of the entire family. Alms and parishioner dues, as well as the income from sutra recitation, make it possible to train and feed monks gratis. And because others make the "awakened way" financially possible, a deep understanding of interdependency and gratitude fuels the monks' practice—a practice that does not end with oneself, but affects and includes those who have made one's very practice possible.

Outside of the Asian Buddhist population in the United States, a devotional sense, or a Bodhisattva Way of Zen practice as lived by Maura, has not been considered vital to Zen training until recently. In the early years, we were very enthusiastic about zazen, meditation. We couldn't conceive of real Zen practice as being anything else. Religious ceremonies and daily rituals weren't fully understood. But in actuality, at least half of a Zen teacher's life is devoted to the Bodhisattva Way.

Maura's practice was formed from both these halves—of zazen and the Bodhisattva Way, meditation and sacrifice. Her journals are a poignant record of this practice and will make Maura's unique understanding available for the benefit of others. The Buddhadarma as lived by an Irish-American female monk is now a part of modern Zen history.

Once renunciation and the awakened mind have been fully realized, the way to Buddhahood is clear. Liberation is complete and such liberated beings are then bodhisattvas and buddhas: "enlightened ones," or "empty dwellers." Their usefulness to others both before and after their physical death, is impossible to conceive. They are nothing but useful energy leading to liberation for all beings still caught in conditioned existence.

—from a tattered, anonymous page of copy kept long years ago, when any Dharma in English was rare and precious.

—Patricia Dai-En Bennage

Photograph taken in April 1980

Creaking to the post office
on my rusty bike
I saw one purple iris
wild in the wet green
of the rice field.
I wanted to send it to you.
I can only tell you
it was there.

—Maura O'Halloran